How To Write Cheesy Movies

By
Frank Conniff

Published By
Podhouse 90 Press
ISBN: 978-0692958407

Design, Typesetting and Cover Design by Len Peralta

Dedicated to all Screenwriters and aspiring Screenwriters.

(Studio note: We feel this dedication needs to be more likable.)

Dedicated to all Screenwriters, aspiring Screenwriters, and their puppies.

(Studio note: Seems like this dedication should have a broader appeal. It needs to be edgier, more urban.)

Dedicated to all Screenwriters, aspiring Screenwriters, their puppies, and their wisecracking African American sidekicks.

(Studio note: We'd like the dedication to also be female-centric.)

Dedicated to all Screenwriters, aspiring Screenwriters,
their puppies, their wisecracking African American sidekicks,
and their female friends.

(Studio note: Can the female friend be changed to a guy?)

Dedicated to all Screenwriters, aspiring Screenwriters,
their puppies, their wisecracking African American sidekicks,
and their male friends.

(Studio note: Does it have to be a dedication?)

CHAPTER ONE

What exactly is a cheesy movie? In the *Mystery Science Theater 3000* theme song, you hear the words, "We'll send them cheesy movies, the worst we can find," therefore, would it be safe to assume that the movies featured on MST3K episodes were cheesy?

Yes, you are very safe in assuming that. But what is it that makes these films cheesy? On the surface, the overall suckiness would appear to be the major factor. But it's not just that these films suck. The best (or should I say, worst) are fun to watch, if you do it with friends and coworkers, or if you happen to have a lobotomy on the way to the viewing, although enjoying cheesy movies through induced brain damage is unfortunately not covered in most healthcare plans.

These films are religious experiences because they are God-fucking-awful, so they should be respected in the same way that you'd respect a pile of dog shit by not stepping on it.

But in their own way, these cheesy movies are wonderful. A combination of incompetence, laziness and a flagrant lack of talent have resulted in films like *Manos: The Hands Of Fate, Monster-A-Go-Go, The Creeping Terror* and *Beast Of Yucca Flats*. Whatever the flaws of these films, I have been drawn back to them over and over again.

Granted, it was my job to watch them repeatedly. As a writer at *Mystery Science Theater 3000* during the Comedy Central years, I studied these movies frame by frame. It was the kind of education you never get in schools, which is why we should always make a point of reminding ourselves how fucking great schools are.

So cheesy is a good way to describe these films because cheese, like the cinematic art form itself, gives people pleasure, but like the films that aired on MST3K, cheese also causes severe constipation. So, yes, there are bad things about cheesy movies, but I can't help but be a bit of a Pollyanna about cheese: I always see the clogged colon as half full.

What makes a cheesy movie a cheesy movie? There are many different skill sets that go into the making of motion picture — directing, producing, cinematography, editing, set design, costumes, etc, but out of all the various disciplines involved in the craft of film, screenwriting is the only one that I've actually failed at, so naturally it's the one skill I am qualified to teach.

CHAPTER TWO

I have never considered myself an expert at writing screenplays. But after watching more than a hundred cheesy movies over and over and over again during my tenure at *Mystery Science Theater 3000,* I became something of an authority in the field of cheesy screenwriting, or so I thought. When I moved to Los Angeles (MST3K was filmed in Minneapolis in order a maintain a close proximity to all possible Wisconsin references), I found that despite being well versed in the art of awfulness, I was having little success when it came to writing and selling my movie ideas, which many entertainment industry insiders assured me were every bit as bad as the stuff that was getting made. It seemed like many of the films showing in multiplexes were being written by folks who didn't know what the hell they were doing either. So why were those writers Hollywood Hotshots, while I was at best a Silverlake Shithead?

It took me a while, but after a few years I gleaned some wisdom, gained much insight, and finally figured out the key to great artistic expression. But unfortunately I have a short attention span so I forgot all that shit.

During my years in Hollywood, many people noted that I had a hunger for learning. I think they meant a hunger for potatoes-a-gratin, but there is no denying that I have always had a thirst for knowledge. I wanted to drink in the do's and don'ts of cinematic storytelling like a veggie smoothie. But what I ended up with was a booger-colored sludge dribbling down the side of my chin. I looked like I had just been sodomized by the Jolly Green Giant, but that was implausible because I wasn't in any position to have a meeting with anyone so famous.

Obviously, I had a lot to learn about the craft of screenwriting, not to mention the craft of describing things that don't evoke the image of a bird-seye blowjob.

This much I knew: there were no shortcuts. You could only become great through sweat and hard work. Well, that sounded like a total drag, so instead of learning the art of screenwriting I wondered if I could just skip ahead and teach the art of screenwriting. This thought occurred to me because I began to notice that most of the screenwriting manuals I saw in bookstores were written by people without a single produced screenplay to their credit. The books were all filled with helpful features, such as:

"10 Tips For Writing Million Dollars Scripts."

"How To Grab a Reader's Attention On The First Page."

"How To Write a Guaranteed Blockbuster Every Time Without Fail."

"Pro Tips That Will Result In A Script That Brings You Love and Happiness and Ends All Your Personal Problems."

This is when I had a epiphany. I realized that I was a failure and that I'd never know what true joy is and in all likelihood would die alone and unloved.

Wait, that wasn't my epiphany, that was just a mundane everyday thought that I have all the time. No, my revelation was that being such a failure at writing and selling screenplays meant I had what it took to teach other people how to write and sell screenplays.

I've always admired how the authors of these How-To books were willing to reveal million dollar secrets to their readers, yet had no interest in becoming rich and famous themselves. Otherwise, wouldn't they be writing their own Oscar-winning screenplays? No, all they care about is passing that information on to others. It's as if Gandhi himself knew how to write a Gandhi pic, but since he's Gandhi, he's only interested in teaching others how to best write a Gandhi pic. (Since there's already been a Gandhi film, the screenplay would have to be for a sequel: *Gandhi II - The Dead Years*.)

But I am not one of these saintly people who only think of the spec screenplay sales of others. (By the way, in case you're wondering, a "spec" screenplay is a script that you write speculatively as a proposal for a document that will take up space on your hard drive forever.)

Gandhi, it should be noted, did not write screenplays, and neither did Mother Teresa as far as I know, although I'm sure if she did, she probably would have devoted years of service to herself after agents stopped returning her calls and started treating her like a leper.

Like everyone who has worked in Hollywood, I do know what it's like to be treated like a leper, but that had as much to do with my blotchy skin as it did with my inherent un-marketability.

CHAPTER THREE

Among the things I failed at in Hollywood was being a failure, because I did achieve some success writing for television, but when I tried to branch out into feature film writing, I found to my consternation that studio executives did not treat every word I wrote as sacred text. The "suits" did not bow down before my screenplays and worship them as the Holy Bible; in fact, many of them swore on a stack of bibles that my scripts sucked.

Even when I was doing well as a Hollywood TV writer, with gigs on *Sabrina, The Teenage Witch, Invader Zim, The Drew Carey Show* and *The New Tom Green Show* (aptly titled, it was cancelled after only a couple of months, so it was never not new), I still had my heart set on writing big blockbuster feature film screenplays. As a life-long film buff who grew up during a golden age of groundbreaking, iconoclastic cinema, I knew that TV was ultimately a creative dead end, a vast wasteland of formulaic shows like *The Sopranos, Mad Men, Breaking Bad, The Wire,* and *Mystery Science Theater 3000,* which was so lame they even hired me, whereas movies were where Adam Sandler vehicles and the *Expendables* franchise and *Transformers* and *Fast and the Furious* films were being made. Television was a form of mass entertainment, movies were an art form, according to the only kind of wisdom that really matters in Hollywood —conventional wisdom.

So I put some effort into writing screenplays and I got feedback from industry professionals that was quite constructive:

"This sucks," my agent said.

"What total garbage," a development executive opined.

"Stop calling me, asshole," one manager demanded. (This had nothing to do with any script, I was trying to date her.)

Despite all this, I firmly believe that my screenplays had a lot going for them, it's just that they weren't what is referred to in entertainment industry slang as, "good." And so I would never presume to think that I could teach people how to write screenplays that fall into the "good" genre. But what about all the scripts that aren't good? Some of them get made into movies and the writers of these motion pictures live successful, fulfilling lives, so instead of being jealous of those fuckers, why not became a successful writer of cheesy movies so you can become one of the successful fuckers that other people are jealous of? Just imagine how wonderful it will feel knowing that your peers are sad because you have what they want. If that's not the definition of success in show business, I don't know what is. (My point — I don't know what the definition of success in show business is.)

Nevertheless, the area of cheesy movies is where my particular set of skills come in, and unlike Liam Neeson in *Taken* and *Taken 2, 3, 4, 5, 6, 7, 8, 9, 10, 11, 12* and *14* (he's superstitious), my particular set of skills are of no particular use to anyone, which is why I believe I have what it takes to be a screenwriting instructor.

CHAPTER FOUR

When life gives me lemons, I throw them out and buy a Diet Coke because I prefer that over lemonade. In other words, there is something inside my soul that told me I could turn my knowledge of bad movies into a force for good.

And then came my Eureka moment. I was driving through Eureka, Nevada when I remembered that my experience on *Mystery Science Theater 3000* gave me a tutorial in cheesy screenwriting that most people never get the opportunity to have (most people are very, very grateful that they've never had this opportunity). The films featured on *Mystery Science Theater 3000* are among the worst ever made, and that's saying a lot, considering that we live in a world where *The Emoji Movie* is an actual thing. And say what you will about the folks who wrote the films that were featured, riffed and ridiculed on *Mystery Science Theater 3000,* they can proudly and unequivocally declare something that few other people can claim: "My screenplay was produced."

We sometimes forget that the core of a cheesy movie is a cheesy screenplay. It has been noted in other instructional books about film that it is hard to make a good movie from a bad screenplay. For instance, when he was filming his *Star Wars* prequels, George Lucas had all the technology and money he needed to make whatever films he wanted. There was nothing holding him back from greatness except for the inconvenient truth that the scripts he wrote weren't all that great. As a result, *Star Wars* fans only watched those prequels about five or six times and then only purchased

20

one or two editions of the Blu-Ray DVDs. And Lucas, who had such high hopes for his dream project, walked away only a few billion dollars richer. It is a sad story indeed. But if Lucas had never put the work into those cheesy scripts, he never would have been able to make those cheesy movies. There's a lesson to be learned from this. I have no idea what in God's name that lesson is, so maybe I'm not being particularly helpful, but just be glad I haven't written any prequels to this book. *Yet.*

Keep in mind, your cheesy screenplay will not be looked forward to and highly anticipated the way the *Star Wars* prequels were. Fans literally slept in the streets for months so that they could be disappointed before anyone else. Other fans had to change their outlooks and get used to the idea that popular entertainment was sometimes not popular or entertaining. But since it was *Star Wars*, people just couldn't accept this, so they went again and again, hoping that by the ninth or tenth viewing it would finally start to get good. They soon found out, however, that movies, like people, are reluctant to change.

But even if you can't get people exited about your cheesy screenplay the way George Lucas did, you'll never get people to come see your cheesy movie unless you write it in the first place. Remember, writing a cheesy screenplay that becomes a cheesy movie is a way to become part of the national conversation, even if that conversation is mostly about how much you suck.

When it comes to cheesy movies, cheesy screenplays are the most essential ingredient, although it certainly doesn't hurt to have a bad cast and an incompetent director. But a bad script does not necessarily encourage people to do their worst work; in fact, most actors give it everything they've got regardless of the material they're given. Many filmmakers and craftspeople approach every project, good or bad, with the utmost professionalism. But don't let these devoted artists distract from your job, which is to write the cheesiest possible screenplay. The fear that it might turn out better than you imagined could paralyze you before you even get started, so try not to think about it. Have faith in your own mediocrity.

CHAPTER FIVE

If it's impossible to fashion a good movie from a bad script, it is also hard to produce a bad movie from a good screenplay, although there are a lot of things that can go wrong in the making of a film. Even the greatest screenplay ever written can turn bad if the film is miscast. What if instead of Jack Nicholson, Scott Baio had been given the lead in *Chinatown*? That would have been wrong because, for one thing, he would have been too young, and also, as an actor, he's the kind of person that in Stanislavskian terms can best be described as a stupid fuckwad. And it should go without saying (but it won't), that casting Faye Dunaway as Joanie in *Joanie Loves Chachi* might have made it better, and yet thank God this never happened. Faye Dunaway is a great actress, so the last thing she should be subjected to is Scott Baio's cooties.

Chinatown is an acclaimed film written by Robert Towne. It won an Academy Award for Best Screenplay, but there are flaws. For instance, the movie is called *Chinatown*, yet there is maybe like one scene in the whole story that takes place in Chinatown. It's supposed to be a metaphor or some shit like that, but don't let that worry you: lots of movies have been written without metaphors, or even characters and stories for that matter. But the good news for you is that Robert Towne's willingness to call a film *Chinatown* that doesn't take place in Chinatown means you have license to call your movie whatever the hell you like. This will help make your script that much more marketable. For instance, if you've written a screenplay about people dying of starvation during a famine in Bangladesh, why not call it, "Boobs-a-Poppin?" Sure, it has nothing to do with your story, but the most acclaimed screenplay of all time was called *Chinatown* and it didn't even take place in friggin' Chinatown, so big whup.

Another important tip to learn from the *Chinatown* script is the importance of streamlining and consolidating characters. You may remember that one of the most famous lines from *Chinatown* is "She's my sister, she's my daughter, she's my sister, she's my daughter, she's my sister AND my daughter!" Notice how they combined two potential characters into one character, thus cutting costs so money that might otherwise have been spent on another actor could be freed up for cocaine (*Chinatown* was made in Hollywood in the 1970s, so I think I'm making a safe assumption here).

Another example of a movie that combined characters is *Robot Monster*. In some circles, it is not as highly regarded as *Chinatown*, but it also streamlines two characters into one character - "I'm a robot, I'm a monster, I'm a robot, I'm a monster, I'm a robot, I'm a monster, I'm a robot AND a monster!"

Without giving anything away, I'll tell you the ending: it turns out the whole thing was a dream. For a screenwriter, this kind of ending serves two purposes:

1. It's an effective way to make sure that regardless of what happens in your story, everything turns out alright for your characters.

2. It's an effective way to tell the audience to go fuck themselves.

Seriously, telling an audience, "it was all a dream" is an example of extracting revenge on paying customers who wish you no ill will. But at least you'll be getting a rise out of them: If you can't entertain moviegoers, the least you can do is piss them off.

You could point out that *The Wizard of Oz* - spoiler warning - turns out to all be a dream, and it is one of the most beloved movies of all time, but that would ruin the premise of my thesis, so please do me a favor and don't point that out.

CHAPTER SIX

How much contempt should a writer of cheesy movies have towards an audience? After all, the end result of your work will probably be one of the following:

An auditorium of bored, irritated people.

A plane passenger who wishes he had purchased that James Patterson novel in the airport.

Someone watching your film on DVD at home and regretting that they are not much, much more drunk.

An individual who tells everyone that he actually likes your movie and then wonders why he doesn't have any friends.

The case could be made that writing a cheesy movie is a hostile act on your part. You could refute this by making the argument that there was an absence of malice, but then you'll be hit with the counter-argument that there was an absence of talent.

An artist has an obligation to share his or her vision with the public, to somehow transform the consciousness of the world. This is a tall order for the writer of cheesy movies because frequently what his or her work induces is unconsciousness.

There is the possibility that once your cheesy movie puts someone to sleep, that person will have an awesome dream that might otherwise have never happened had it not been for the slumber your work induced. Alas, this won't do you much good because it may be true that in dreams begin responsibilities, but unfortunately in the current Writers Guild minimum agreement, a dream that is "based on material from another medium" does not pay residuals.

With all this weighing on a writer's mind, where does the motivation to write come from? One of the great motivators is revenge. When you are writing that touching, heartfelt story that is a celebration of the human spirit, make a point of remembering who you will be getting back at and screwing over.

Will it be the teachers who berated you for being a shitty student?

Or, more specifically, the gym coach who humiliated you for being a poor athlete?

Is it the bullies who made fun of you for being a total jag off even though you knew in your heart of hearts that you were only a partial jag off?

Is it the women or men who rejected you and were so unromantic that they didn't send a box of chocolates along with the restraining order they served you with?

Or was it your parents, who committed the unpardonable sin of feeding you and putting a roof over your head? *(Assholes!)*

The best way to extract revenge on everyone is to write a cheesy movie so that when they see your film, you will make them suffer as much as they made you suffer.

CHAPTER SEVEN

One of the most basic questions of craft that writing instructors are asked is, "Will my writing ever fill the empty gap that lays deep within me like a bottomless sink hole of need? Can success, fame, and wealth ever give me anywhere near the fulfillment that I seek?"

The obvious answer is — fuck no. But writers are always instructed to avoid the obvious. And you should always maintain a level of excited anticipation as you write. If, during the crafting of your script, you can constantly repeat to yourself, "this could very well be the next *Manos: The Hands Of Fate,*" it will keep you going, although where you're going might very well be a meth lab.

In the meantime, you have to study the work of those who came before you. There is lots to be learned from great screenplays, but overall, if you're going to write a cheesy screenplay that sucks ass, you are better off studying scripts that were written in the suck-ass genre, like *The Beast of Yucca Flats, Red Zone Cuba*, and *Skydivers*.

The above films were all written and directed by Coleman Francis. He made three entire pictures and most scholars of cinema agree that he had no idea what the hell he was doing. So he is a role model to aspiring writers of cheesy movies who are worried that knowing what the hell you're doing might be some sort of litmus test.

But surprisingly enough, it turns out that examining the work of a bad screenwriter might be harder than examining the work of a good screenwriter.

I'll explain.

The study of creative endeavors like writing, painting, music and film-making mostly involves the study of craft. But when an artist produces a work with no craftsmanship whatsoever, how are you supposed to study something that isn't there in the first place? This is why Coleman Francis's work is not taught in any university, not even Trump University, and not just because the cinema department of that school mainly specialized in snuff films. Admittedly, Coleman Francis movies seem like snuff films: nobody actually dies in them, but the spirit of the viewer gets snuffed out every time they are watched. Not just anybody can write a Coleman Francis film, it takes a special kind of psychosis. You're either born with it, or it's injected into your brain during a covert military experiment by a rogue black ops unit.

I know from experience that it is a daunting challenge to explain exactly what went into the making of *Beast of Yucca Flats* because I saw that movie a half dozen times and I have absolutely no memory of it except my recollection that I had no idea what was going on as I watched it. So if I can teach you how to create the kind of work that is forgotten even before an audience has finished watching it, I will have given you the skills to produce the cinematic equivalent of a medically induced coma.

Red Zone Cuba had an innovative approach to character development in that it didn't have any. Character development is a key component of any movie. If you can make your characters come alive on the page, you will have a better than average chance of selling your screenplay. But being better than average is a lot to ask of anyone, especially a writer of cheesy movies. Some cheesy writers are capable making their characters leap off the page, but often it is to their deaths.

So how do you develop characters in your script? A lot of screenwriters base the people in their screenplays on characters they see in other movies. This is done by screenwriters both good and bad. The bad ones do it because they have no choice and the good ones do it because studio executives insist upon it. You may have noticed that after the first *Guardians of the Galaxy* movie was a huge hit, suddenly every superhero and sci-fi movie had characters who are really into 1970s pop songs. It happened in *Doctor Strange, Suicide Squad, Alien Covenant, The Martian,* and a few others, and this was only because the main character in *Guardians of the Galaxy* was into 1970s pop songs. I'm glad this wasn't a trend in the early 1990s, otherwise Oskar Schindler in *Schindler's List* might have been portrayed as a huge Loggins & Messina fan and I'm pretty sure that would have been historically inaccurate.

It's important that your main character be likable. You may have noticed that Hannibal Lecter in *Silence of the Lambs* was charming, erudite, had good table manners, and if memory serves, thoughtfully wore a lobster bib when he bit people's faces off.

The screenplay for *Silence of the Lambs* won an Academy Award, so you would think that anyone who wants to take home that trophy would see to it that his or her screenplay has cannibalistic elements in it, but this is not always the case. *Funny Girl,* with Barbara Streisand, won several major awards, but nowhere in the film did you hear the lyric, "People, eating other people, are the luckiest people in the world," although to be fair this movie was released long before *Silence of the Lambs.*

Saving Private Ryan had characters with severed limbs, but none of them were digested during the course of the story, which may have been a missed opportunity: "I'm totally full, I couldn't eat another bite, I'm saving Private Ryan for later when I might want a late night snack" could have been a good way to work the film's title into the dialogue.

But there's more to cheesy movies than cannibalism. I only bring up this up to emphasize the importance of likable characters. These films I just mentioned are prestigious, quality movies, but MST3K-worthy films do not follow the guidelines of prestigious, quality movies. Sometimes the main characters are unlikable just because the films themselves are unlikable.

Godzilla is portrayed as a lovable rogue who fell in with the wrong radiation, but not only does he destroy cities, killing millions of people, but he is aloof and standoffish as he does so, although many people in those crushed buildings would argue that the main problem is that he is too stand-on-ish. But personality-wise, Godzilla really does come across like a remote hipster too cool to care, bemoaning the inauthenticity of any neighborhood that hasn't been reduced to rubble.

One of the most glaring examples of a screenwriter going out of his way to make a character unlikable is in the MST3K-riffed movie *Wild Rebels*. There is a scene where the main character, played by Steve Alaimo, walks into a bar (unfortunately he is not accompanied by a Priest and a Rabbi, so the scene is not funny). He goes up to the bartender and orders a beer. When the bartender, a friendly and affable guy, asks, "what kind of beer?" Steve Alaimo replies with a nasty sneer, "cold."

This little exchange has nothing to do with the story. Its only purpose is to show us that the hero, the guy we're supposed to be rooting for, is kind of a dick. The result is that we now hate the main character and there's still over an hour left in the film to go.

This is cheesy screenwriting at its core. It's the kind of incompetent storytelling that can't be taught, but I'm teaching it anyway because I've got nothing better to do.

Does this seem unnecessarily glib? No, I would say it's necessarily glib, because "I've got nothing better to do" is going to be the main motivation for anyone who ends up seeing your cheesy movie if it gets made. So as a writer of cheesy movies, your job is to tap into the mindset of a person who wants to kill time and doesn't have anything better to do than watch your movie. There are a lot of easily entertained people out there, and if you can somehow exploit their willingness to watch anything that happens to be on, you could end up having a screenwriting career that stands the test of time, providing it's a remedial test.

By the way, William Grefe, who made *Wild Rebels*, had a long career of cheesy screenwriting and directing. A truly independent filmmaker, he directed all of his movies in Florida, without any apparent desire to come make films here in America. His screenplay for *Wild Rebels* was as cheesy as they come, and his other films, with titles like *Death Curse of Tartu, The Devil's Sisters* and *The Hooked Generation*, would seem to indicate that he devoted the entirety of his filmography to cheesy movie-making. He was a genuine maverick, working outside the studio system and remaining a regional filmmaker for his whole career. Wealth and fame eluded him, but despite everything, he did leave behind a body or work, and I find that quite admirable.

I talk a lot in this book about getting an agent, selling your cheesy screenplay and working in Hollywood, William Grefe went the do-it-yourself route and this was all before the age of digital filmmaking and making movies on your iPhone. He was part of a generation of independent filmmakers that had to lug big cameras and haul bulky equipment to their shoots. It was an exhausting process not just for feature filmmakers, but also for the directors of shorter, more idiosyncratic movies, like Bob Crane.

In the 1950s, 1960s, and 1970s, indy film mostly meant cheesy film. This can still be the case, but it's up to you. If you've written a cheesy movie, and you have an iPhone, you have the option of going out and making it on your own, and these days that is much more doable than when William Grefe was doing it himself.

Do you have film-nerd friends with knowledge of lighting and sound who would like to start building a resume? Do you know men and women who are total hams and would be happy to spend a few weekends covered in blood and screaming for the camera with the possibility of future movie stardom as their only payment? If so, send them your cheesy screenplay, promise them free cheesy snacks, and make it happen.

CHAPTER EIGHT

In order for a screenplay to have wisdom and maturity, it has to appeal to a younger audience. You know who I'm talking about — the kids today with their hula hoops and crazy music.

How to go about grabbing the youth market? It wouldn't hurt to pepper your script with catch phrases that younger movie-goers can relate to. In the screenplays I've written, characters are always saying cool shit like, "groovy" and "far out." This hasn't resulted in a sale or a screenwriting career, but it has qualified me for AARP discounts.

In the old days, the way to appeal to youth was to put the word "teenage" into a title. MST3K-riffed movies are lousy with teenage titles: *Teenage Crime Wave, Teenagers From Outer Space, High School Big Shot* (the "High School" in the title implies teenage, although I was in my late-twenties when I finally got my diploma, and by diploma I mean equivalency, and by equivalency I mean Arby's Trainee badge).

Calling Robert Vaughn a "teenage" caveman is a bit of a stretch. As much as I love Vaughn as an actor, in *Teenage Caveman* he looked like a dad accompanying his kid to an *It's About Time* cosplay convention (I could have gone with a *2000 Years BC,* or a *Quest For Fire* reference there, but as you might already know, I'm a bit self-destructive when it comes to pop culture references.)

Have you finished googling *It's About Time*? Okay, let's move on.

The lifespan of a Caveman was short back in those prehistoric days. The world was so new, nothing had a chance to be retro yet. Hipster Cavemen considered those who used fire to be total sell-outs, and they made a point of using "vintage" chisels when they carved cave drawings, which they bragged had an "indy sensibility." These prehistoric poseurs were met with blank stares, and the fact that all the twigs and branches they ate were locally grown did not mean much.

As you all know, hipsters are every bit as insufferable now as they were then. There are modern music snobs who have nothing but disdain for *The Brady Bunch* and *Gilligan's Island* theme songs, feeling that Sherwood Schwartz hadn't written anything valid since his *It's About Time* theme song. (I have no idea why I brought this up, except to throw another completely irrelevant *It's About Time* reference into the mix, and also to point out that I guess I am one of those hipster music snobs who brags about being into early Sherwood Schwartz TV theme songs before they were cool.)

But back to the subject of *Teenage Caveman*, it is a fact that a caveman who was a teenager had pretty much reached the halfway point in his life. Archeologists have uncovered evidence that in Paleolithic times, the qualifying age for half-price senior citizen groupons was twenty-five, but calling the movie Middle Aged Caveman would have been far less marketable, although more accurate. So let this be a lesson to you: if anything in your script ever seems accurate or true to life, remove it immediately.

Regardless of how young or old your characters are, or how real or unreal your story is, there is no better insurance for a cheesy movie than a cheesy screenplay. And since so many cheesy movies are produced every year, the good news is that there's a growing market for scripts written by people who have no business writing them in the first place.

But is it my business to say who has any business writing a script? Do I have the right to say who should and shouldn't pursue a writing career? I'll put the answer in writing: no. But if you're like me, you don't need an outside voice of discouragement to crush your dreams; that voice is already right there, deep within yourself, the accumulated result of years and years of passive-aggressive friends, emotionally abusive family members, resentful authority figures, and backstabbers from all walks of life who have implanted time-release bombs of doubt into your psyche.

But you need to cast away all that noise and rely solely on your own negativity and your own low self-esteem. It's not enough to be a depressed writer, your goal is to be a successful depressed writer, and in order to achieve this, you have to be able to spend all day not getting out of bed on your own two feet.

I am just trying to unlock the storage freezer inside your brain. I can open doors for you, and not just because I am such a failure as a screen-writer that I work part-time as a doorman, but also in the sense that I can teach the basics of unsuccessful screenwriting in a way that only seriously unsuccessful screenwriters can.

That's right, I am admitting to myself and to others that I was an unsuccessful screenwriter. Being openly truthful about a painful personal failure can be a healing experience that removes a weight from your psyche and liberates your soul. That certainly isn't the case here; I feel worse than ever now that I've said it out loud. But if I'm being honest with myself, I have to admit that being honest with myself really sucks.

However, before we go forward, I must emphasize that no matter what kind of a script you write, there is all sorts of wisdom and and many kinds of pro-tips that have been assembled through the years that can be helpful to any kind of person doing any kind of writing.

Does anybody know what these are? Seriously, this book would be much more useful if I knew any of that shit.

CHAPTER NINE

There is a better than average chance that not many people are clamoring to unlock the creative secrets behind the MST3K-riffed movie, *Beast of Yucca Flats*. But can writing something like *Beast Of Yucca Flats* really be taught? Explaining the process by which feces is formed would require a learned scientist with a scholarly knowledge of poop, and by the same token, any study of *Beast Of Yucca Flats* would involve a detailed medical understanding of the bacterial infections that result from Coleman Francis films. Most teachers of cinema studies are hindered by their longtime exposure to movies of quality, but you can't watch as many MST3K films as many times as I have without gleaning some wisdom about the art of quality-free filmmaking. So here is what I think is the first thing you should do if you want to write a movie that will one day be considered cheesy enough to be riff-worthy by *Mystery Science Theater 3000:*

Take a gigantic dump on the floor. (Do this on purpose, not accidentally, as is happening more and more often to this writer.) Look at it. Study it. Smell it. Try to absorb its essence. I'm not saying smear it all over yourself because this is cheesy screenwriting we're talking about, not performance art. Also, you're a writer trying to break into the movie business, not Ted Nugent trying to avoid serving in the military. But if you can somehow translate the emotions evoked by a hot steaming pile of dung and get it down on writing paper the same way you'd get the actual feces down on toilet paper, you may have the necessary skills to write a script that isn't even remotely *Chinatown.*

But as hard as this is to accept, you may have to grapple with a harsh reality that some would-be writers of cheesy movies have to face: maybe you are just not capable of writing a boring movie. Please don't take this the wrong way, but it could turn out that you are too interesting and talented to write a screenplay that inflicts an hour and a half of tedium on the world.

But all is not lost. If you can't write a boring movie, you can at least write a confusing one. Inception was proof that confusion can be the stuff of blockbusters. I won't go into detail about *Inception* because lots of people were entertained by it and the film made a fortune for the author of its screenplay, Christopher Nolan. I found the film to be such a labyrinth of what-the-fuck that my head exploded, and this may very well be what gave Nolan the idea for *Dunkirk*. So I'm not going to dwell on Mr. Nolan's work too much, because in our ongoing dispute, he always wins.

So instead of *Inception*, I will dwell on *Castle of Fu Manchu*. (Damn it, Nolan wins again!). *Castle of Fu Manchu* sets up its story by having a bunch of crap happen even though there is no story. And then, some more crap happens and... other things, and then... Oh, Christ, please make me stop thinking about this film! Did I even watch it, or did Leo DiCaprio implant it into my dreams so that I'd go insane? (Another victory for Chris Nolan!)

Castle of Fu Manchu was featured on an episode of *Mystery Science Theater 3000*, and most of us considered it not so much a movie as a portal into the abyss. It wasn't the most poorly made film we ever did, not by a long shot. It had a pretty decent sized budget and there were good actors in it. There is no reason for this movie to be the film that many on the MST3K writing staff agree was the worst we ever found, but it was, and all the credit for that can specifically be traced to its absolutely incomprehensible cheesy screenplay.

Watching that film was like being slipped roffies at an InfoWars office party. We didn't understand or follow even one thing that happened in the movie. But the guy who wrote the script got paid actual money for it, and I am certain of one thing: writing *Castle of Fu Manchu* could not have been nearly as painful as watching *Castle of Fu Manchu*.

Making an unsuccessful Fu Manchu movie was quite an accomplishment because audiences who love racism have long been fans of this popular franchise. But the script was so convoluted and incoherent that the racial stereotypes and cartoonish villainy normally so delightful to movie-goers was lost within the depraved opium hallucination that tried to pass itself off as a plot.

Writing a script this cheesy is challenging, but you don't have to dive in head first, although diving in head first might give you a brain injury that will put you in the proper frame of mind as you are developing the screenplay.

CHAPTER TEN

And now the time has come to discuss the foundation for the condemned house you are going to build.

I'm talking about your screenplay's outline.

The first thing I need to tell you is that once you sit down to write the outline, make sure you type it up as neatly as possible. I once wrote an outline in crayon, but agents and development executives saw this for what it was - an attempt to make my story seem more sophisticated than it actually was. So don't try any tricks or deceptions to make your work come off as something that it's not. Let the cheesiness of your story speak for itself. You don't want the cheap tricks and contrivances that you're using to sell your script to distract from the cheap tricks and contrivances that are actually in your script.

When I submitted that outline in crayon, I thought I was being clever, but I was actually committing an act of self-sabotage. But it should be noted that if you're setting out to become any kind of writer, self-sabotage is already an integral part of your life. Let's face it, you sabotaged yourself by becoming a writer in the first place, but actively undermining your chances of succeeding is a skill in of itself. Not every writer has the capacity to be one's own worst enemy. Some are born with an innate ability to follow through on the goals they set out for themselves, and some even have social skills, which is a freakish occurrence in a writer, but believe it or not there are documented cases of writers interacting with others in non-awkward ways, but these instances are so few and far between they are not worth mentioning.

However, if you are the other, more common kind of writer, the kind that is on a slow-moving collision course with an abyss of your own making, the best I can do is give you a few tips that will help you get in your own way.

First of all, never miss an opportunity to shoot yourself in the foot. I don't mean this literally; actually shooting yourself in the foot will make people think you tried to kill yourself, but didn't take it to the next level. Therefore, they might suspect you of being undependable if they hired you to work on a project. No one respects an artist who does a half-assed job. Writers like Sylvia Plath and Ernest Hemingway finished what they started, which is why they are still in such demand. Sometimes, to achieve true success, you have to be willing to achieve it posthumously.

But, please - never, never, never kill yourself under any circumstances. I think the writers who took this drastic step might have lived longer lives had they not committed suicide. Also, the word "suicide" is now the title of a cheesy movie - *Suicide Squad* - so if you ascend into an afterlife it might very well turn out to be a DC Universe, and that's a cosmic punishment nobody deserves. And I'll also point out that I have been near-suicidal a few times in my life, and had I gone through with my darkest impulses, I wouldn't be here writing this book. (It strikes me that this is not the best argument against suicide, but still, I stand by what I said — a cheesy life is still a life worth living.)

Shooting yourself in the foot is also problematic because if you're a cheesy writer, you'll be hard-pressed to come up with a metaphor for what you just did. In other words, to put it in the only way I am capable of putting it — if you shoot yourself in the foot you'll really be shooting yourself in the foot.

Perhaps the most effective form of self-sabotage for a writer is not writing. Not writing is a goal that many writers aspire to, but when you're starting out as a writer, not writing is in some ways counter-productive. Having nothing to show for what you've done is a luxury only those in the highest rungs of the entertainment industry are allowed to enjoy. So you have to write, and since you are an un-produced, out-of-work writer, you need to be nice to people despite being in an irritable mood because you have to spend at least part of your day writing.

Being a total dick in social situations with people who can help your career is another form of self-sabotage, but the chances that you'll meet someone in this position are slim, so in the meantime it might be a good idea to practice being a dick towards ordinary, everyday people. What's an effective way to be a dick towards ordinary, everyday people? Well, you might start by making a point of telling them how ordinary and everyday they are.

But you can also go too far in the opposite direction: overdoing it when you kiss up to people can be just as harmful as telling them to go fuck themselves. Don't get me wrong: you are going to have to kiss up to people. As you prepare to navigate your way through the entertainment industry, it's a good a idea to practice fake-laughing and nodding your head in agreement with people you have nothing but contempt for. But it's impolite to stick your nose all the way up somebody's ass unless you've already scheduled an appointment with their anus. And once you are in that studio executive's office and your nostrils are covered in shit and you've degraded yourself in every possible way just to get your script sold, there is still one important, universal truth that you must never forget.

Make sure to get your parking validated.

CHAPTER ELEVEN

Okay, you've written your outline and you can't make heads or tails out of what's been put down on paper. You have no idea what you've done, you might as well have written it while you were blackout drunk. Maybe you did write it when you were blackout drunk. Under oath in a court of law you couldn't tell a jury what your story is about or what it means.

If this is the case, congratulations! Your cheesy outline is done and you are ready to move to the next stage of your incoherent itinerary.

The time has come to tackle Act One of your screenplay. This means that your script is now on the one yard line. And it also means some other things that are metaphors for competition, but, sorry, that's about all the sports references you're going to get out of me.

Act One is an important part of the creative process; it is often the first step towards abandoning your script altogether and never getting anything done. Sure, some industry professionals feel that it's hard to get a script produced if you don't finish it in the first place, but that's an out-of-date, analog way of thinking. However, as much of a pain in the ass as it is, completing a screenplay can in certain cases be a valuable part of your methodology and we will at least give lip service to it in this book.

It's also worth pointing out that finishing a script is the best part of writing because it means no more writing. The most satisfying part of the process is when there is no longer any process.

Procrastination is the enemy of all writers, and one of these days I'm going to write an essay on this topic. But the great thing about writing is that once you're finished, you are no longer procrastinating.

Dorothy Parker once said, "I hate writing, I love having written." Miss Parker was a writer of fiction and light verse who had nothing but contempt for the practice of screenwriting. Yet she worked on the screenplays for two first rate movies — the original 1937 version of *A Star Is Born,* and the Alfred Hitchcock thriller, *Saboteur.* Both of these are non-cheesy movies, much higher up on the cinematic food chain than what is mostly being discussed in this book. I could try to give you tips on how to emulate Dorothy Parker in your approach to screenwriting, but you are just a beginner; it requires years of experience to attain the level of skill you'll need to have complete disdain for what you do.

The joy of not writing is something a prolific author like Stephen King will never understand. For years he has placed a premium on productivity. When he completes a project, all he can think to do is start another one. And with each book and screenplay, his writing becomes more eloquent and articulate, but on the other hand, I haven't written nearly as many books as Stephen King has, yet being eloquent and articulate is a total thing with me.

There is always the option of hiring someone to do all your writing. This is how Donald Trump, a man who has never read a book, became the author of a book. But you probably are not wealthy enough to choose this option, and I'm going to give you the benefit of the doubt and say that you're probably not evil enough, either.

And there are other considerations besides money to keep in mind. Firstly, at this stage of your nascent career, you can't afford to skip a step, and thirdly, whomever you hire most likely doesn't want to do any writing either, and that means getting him or her to meet a deadline is going to be a bitch.

So don't put it off. You should immediately sit down and without hesitation figure out a time in three or four weeks when you can start writing.

And once that awful day comes, you may think it means you have to begin on page one, but your starting point is actually the title page. Pretty much all the professional scripts I've read had title pages. You can make a good movie with a bad title, as the makers of *The Shawshank Redemption* will attest, but the proper title will indicate to audiences the tone of the film. Moviegoers looking for a solemn and prestigious drama were kept away by the title *Booty Call*, despite the gravitas inherent in its story. And audiences in need of a fun filled romp packed with lots of bootylishious fuckin' avoided *Remains of the Day*, which is a shame, because that is a damn good movie.

Sometimes a writer can be intimidated when he or she comes up with a title that makes the story seem really cool, and then you can't come up with anything cool to happen in the actual film. The MST3K-riffed movie *Star Fighters* has a cool name, but most of it was just jets in the sky refueling. I give them credit for just outright showing two jets refueling and not tiptoeing around the subject matter by showing scenes of people having sex. It's like when I watch a porno, all I can think is, come on, quit dilly dallying with these shots of people having intercourse and just get to the part where the train goes through a tunnel.

Your cheesy screenplay will contain many elements, but one thing it almost certainly will not have is redeeming social value. Therefore, we should take a moment to wonder if writing porn is an option for the aspiring screenwriter, the theory being, if you can write a cheesy movie, why not a sleazy movie?

It's a close call, but ultimately my verdict is that writing sleazy is a step down from writing cheesy. The graphic moments in porno films slow the plot down, but as a writer of cheesy screenplays, your job is to slow the plot down without having to rely on sex scenes. If you really know what you're doing, the plot will have come to a complete standstill in the first moment of your story, and then it's up to you to make sure the pace never picks up. As a writer of cheesy movies, you do banal, not anal.

Also, porn gives people pleasure, something that can't be said for many of the films that were riffed on episodes of *Mystery Science Theater 3000*.

Ultimately, sleaze and cheese are completely different genres.

One other thing. If you go by the edict that you should write what you know, a film involving characters having lots of sex will not reflect the life of a broke and unemployed writer.

So what should the title of your screenplay be? For a while I was naming all of my scripts, *Untitled Frank Conniff Project*. It made my screenplays seem important, at least the "untitled" and "project" part. But in general, it's not a good idea to put your name in a title, unless your name is Spider Man, but then you will eventually become exhausted from rebooting yourself over and over again. Your best option is to come up with a title that doesn't have your name in it, and your title could even have something to do with the story you are trying to tell, if you don't want to go the Chinatown route.

What's a good title for a movie? Let's look at the case of *Manos: The Hands of Fate*, even though we are under no legal obligation to do so. What did the title *Manos: The Hands of Fate* have to do with the story? Nobody has any fucking idea, but Harold P. Warren, the writer of the Manos script, clearly thought this was the title to go with. However, he is not the person to consult about anything having to do with *Manos: The Hands of Fate* for the simple reason that he is the person who wrote *Manos the Hands of Fate* and as thus cannot be trusted about matters having to do with *Manos: The Hands of Fate*.

Still, readers of this book should do everything they can to emulate him. I'm not saying you have what it takes to write the next *Manos: The Hands of Fate* - that kind of incoherent, incompetent storytelling is something that can't be taught, it's something you are born with, like Type-1 diabetes.

But what's inspiring about Harold P. Warren is that he wasn't a Hollywood professional, he was a Texas fertilizer salesman. This might make you wonder if having experience in the business of making shit is necessary when it comes to the business of writing shit, but please take heart — people from all walks of life, not just fertilizer salesmen, have written pieces of shit.

What would have been a better title than *Manos: The Hands of Fate*? Basically any title you can think of, like for instance, *Mother May I Sleep With Danger?* (An unfair comparison, because that is the greatest title for any movie ever.)

Mitchell was a great title because the main character was named Mitchell. *Mitchell!* It kind of rolls off the tongue, doesn't it? And since this is Mitchell we're talking about, that tongue is engulfed in toxic levels of halitosis, not to mention the aftershocks of multiple bratwurst burps.

Naming your script after a character in the story is usually a good option. Besides Mitchell, other examples include *Mary Poppins, Michael Clayton, Erin Brockovitch*, and *Beastmaster* (haven't seen that movie in a while, but I believe his full name was Marvin Breastmaster if I recall correctly).

The one thing you don't want to have is spoilers in your title. *Citizen Kane* is generally acknowledged to be a great title for a great movie, which is why calling it *A Sled Named Rosebud* would have been a mistake. The same goes for changing the title of *The Sixth Sense* to *The Man Who Was Dead The Whole Time*.

The only successful property I can think of where they gave away the ending in the title was *Death of a Salesman,* but since there were no sequels and it never became any kind of blockbuster tentpole movie property, it's a good bet that Arthur Miller eventually realized that both the title and the ending were a mistake.

Unfortunately, these kinds of miscalculations hindered Miller throughout his career. He somehow neglected to turn *The Crucible* into a lucrative franchise, even though it had witches in it, and as Miller's dramatic idol, August Strindberg, once said, witches are friggin' cool! The main characters in *The Crucible* were burned at the stake, but since they were witches, Miller could have brought them back for spinoffs and sequels. I guess he was too busy sleeping with Marlyn Monroe to exploit the Dark Universe he had created. I mean, why kill off a bunch of awesome sexy witches without leaving open the option of having them come back to haunt and cast spells on people?

But it wasn't just *The Crucible*. Arthur Miller never even tried to turn his Holocaust drama *Playing For Time* into a video game, even though it already had the word "playing" in its title.

This whole topic is worrisome for readers of this book because if a Pulitzer Prize winner like Arthur Miller can be so careless when it comes to cashing in on his own work, imagine how hard this shit is going to be for you.

CHAPTER TWELVE

Okay, so you've come up with a title, you've typed it in the middle of a page or maybe used one of those fancy Final Draft software programs where there's a title page already set up for you. This has always been an intimidating subject for a non-techie like myself, because software is all done with computers now. But software can be a big help with formatting, although you still have to come up with the plot, story, characters and situations yourself, so they're not perfect. As of this writing, Final Draft, Scriptware, Master Writer and Hack Helper are the major screenwriting computer programs. (Actually, the last one is an app that I'm developing and by "developing," I mean I just thought of it.). All of these systems make big promises, but in my experience, none of them do the actual writing for you, so they're pretty useless.

A few years ago someone did invent a computer that was programmed to write a script, and in fact the programmer did an amazing job of simulating a real writer, even to the point where the computer spent a lot of time avoiding writing and devoting a large amount of energy to resenting Arron Sorkin and wishing failure on Lena Dunham. The computer also became so self-aware that it started going to Hollywood coffee shops where it wore a baseball cap backwards and tried to write scripts, but spent most of the day using the free wi-fi to surf the internet. It was given one of the most advanced artificial intelligences ever in the hopes that its probing mind would unlock the mysteries of art and creativity. But all it ended up ever asking was, "Do you know how I can get an agent?"

By the way, in case you didn't know, coffee shops in Hollywood cater to screenwriters who work on their scripts away from home. One cafe that I spent time at had a daily special - half-priced scones for writers with second act problems.

But even a computer from the future that goes back in time to kill the leader of the resistance has to come up with a story if it's going to write a screenplay. And if you're a member of the human species, inventing a plot for a script will require all the creativity and inventiveness at your disposal.

So yeah, you're pretty much fucked.

CHAPTER THIRTEEN

To author a screenplay, you first need a story, right? In some cases, yes. So where do you find stories? The best source is ordinary, everyday life. In the course of your daily existence, there are probably interesting incidents and events happening all around you. So make a point of ignoring them and instead look for the one dull, pointless story that only you can tell.

Big time Hollywood writers get their stories from real life. The guy who wrote *The Walking Dead* one day happened to notice there was a zombie apocalypse going on in his neighborhood. So he based his story on real life, although he did have to change some names. Anyone who can feed off flesh and suck the life out of others is well suited for the movie business, so if you meet a zombie, don't kill it, give it your business card.

Some zombie movies like *Shaun of the Dead*, and *Zombieland* are actually good, but believe it or not, there are also lots of non-zombie cheesy movies based on real life. The guy who wrote *Mitchell* knew a smelly bloated drunk guy and then thought to himself, "What if he were a cop who narc'd on his girlfriends?" The appeal of a story such as this was undeniable, and audiences have been denying it ever since.

Some might be wondering: if ideas come from real life, what happens if I meet a real life person with a great idea, and I steal it from him? Does that mean I've taken an idea from real life?

No, it just means that you've taken an idea. And you should never, ever steal an idea. It is unethical to do so, but more to the point, it's dumb because there's a much safer and more legal form of thievery - it's called being derivative. It's legal, accepted and commonplace, and derivative-ness is the foundation upon which all hackery is built, so listen carefully, or, more appropriately, look over the shoulder and appropriate the notes of the guy sitting next to you who listened carefully.

Above all, you have to be artful in the way you rip-off ideas. For instance, don't write a script called *Star Wars* and then use all the same characters and situations from that film. No, instead, call your movie, *Star Police Action,* or *War in Space,* or *Galaxy Conflict.* If you really want to cover your ass, call it something like, *To Darth Maul, Thanks For Everything, Julie Newmar.*

But just as important, don't give your Star Wars rip-off characters names like Luke Skywalker, Darth Vader, Boba Fett, and especially not Julie Newmar This could possibly tip people off that you're up to something fishy. So instead give your characters names like Duke Cloudstroller, or Foot Soho, or Darth Brooks, or Boba Felt. This will fool everyone, with the possible exception of people who are awake.

And if you are clueless enough to call your villain Darth Vader, tell people that you named him after a guy who lives down the hall from you, not the character from Star Wars But then again, your neighbor might sue you, so take the time to come up with a cool original sci-fi villain name, like Larry Goldberg.

Be careful, because even writers who are merely being derivative do sometimes get sued for plagiarism. Often, successful films end up with some disgruntled nobody filing a lawsuit because he was the one who submitted the idea to a relative of a friend of the assistant to a guy who knew a girl who slept with a dude who once met the trainer of the wife of the person who once valet parked the car of the writer of that big successful film.

If a film is a blockbuster, there's always some schmuck who claims, "Hey, I'm the guy who came up with the premise of *The Terminator.*" (Actually, that guy was Harlan Ellison, and he proved his case and was paid a settlement.)

Harlan Ellison is a brilliant and iconic writer of fiction, and he wrote *City On The Edge Of Forever*, perhaps my all-time favorite *Star Trek* episode. But he is also one of the credited writers of a film from 1966 called

The Oscar, which I love and consider to be one of the cheesiest movies ever made. Good writers work on cheesy movies for different reasons. Some do it for money, others do it for money, but I only bring this up to point out that if you write a cheesy movie that gets produced, you will be in good company.

In a documentary that I saw, Mr. Ellison said that on the night of the premiere of *The Oscar*, he knew that his feature film writing career was over. So don't give up your dreams; if it can happen to him, it can happen to you!

CHAPTER FOURTEEN

We've already established that at some point, one way or another, you are going to have to sit down and start writing. When it comes to the tortuous task of putting words down on paper, Gustave Flaubert probably put it best when he said that the daunting task of writing Madame Bovary, "sucked every kind of ass." (I'm paraphrasing.)

My point is that you are not the first writer to view writing as a worst case scenario. If there was a way to write without actually writing, believe me, somebody would have already written a book about it.

Right now is probably as good a time as any to tell you about the concept of Show Don't Tell. This dictum is a part of every book that teaches good writing, but it might have some applications to this book as well.

What writing instructors mean by Show Don't Tell is: show us your story through action, not by telling us. A good example of Show Don't Tell are the Gamera movies, which were mainstays of not just Japanese monster movies, but flying turtle films in general. In the first of the series, the idea that Gamera is a friend to children is very important to the plot. So the filmmakers SHOW us lots of scenes with Gamera and some weird kid hanging out and being friends. This is SHOWN to us. Of course, this comes after certain characters TELLING us "Gamera is a friend to children" about a million times. In fact, the idea that Gamera is a friend to children would have completely escaped my notice if they hadn't said it out loud. Otherwise my main impression of Gamera would have been just a big-ass turtle who destroys cities and lets a kid talk to him once or twice before resuming his murderous rampage.

Okay, I guess Gamera is a bad Show Don't Tell example.

But they did show us scenes of Gamera flying and destroying scale models of cities, which Japanese monster movies have taught us is every bit as tragic as destroying real cities. If they had not shown these scenes of carnage but instead had a scene of a character in a room describing everything that happened, it wouldn't have been nearly as effective, especially when you consider how poorly dubbed it would have been. So SHOWING scale model cities destroyed by guys in rubber suits is much more powerful than TELLING us about scale model cities being destroyed by guys in rubber suits.

But whether you're showing or telling, all screenwriters have the same goal: getting their scripts produced, and having their films become so successful that they get promoted to producer or director and then they no longer have to write anymore. Why write when you can lord it over other writers and tell them what to write? Hollywood is filled with people who've never written anything ever, yet have millions of opinions about what other people should be writing.

There was a time in America's past when people aspired to write the Great American Novel. Then, as film culture grew, people wanted to write the Great American Screenplay. In recent years this has evolved into people wanting to give notes on the Great American Screenplay.

Writers love to imagine this dream come true: someone else has to do the degrading chore of writing, and you are the one who gets to commit the ultimate act of creativity — judging and criticizing other people's work.

If you're a director, you can spend the rest of your life not putting one word to paper and yet you are still allowed to have it say "a film by" at the beginning of your film. That is one sweet deal.

This is not to say that some non-writing directors aren't creative forces, and the fact that they can achieve this without doing any writing is something all writers should admire. Many aspiring screenwriters dream of one day being so good and so successful that only the best filmmakers in the business take credit for their ideas.

You may have heard of "the auteur theory." It is a theory that posits the notion that directors are always the sole author of a film, regardless of who else might be involved. In case you didn't know, "auteur" is a French word meaning, "pretentious narcissist taking all the credit."

But none of this matters because for now at least, you are stuck with the miserable task of typing words onto a computer screen. There are some writers who prefer writing longhand in a moleskin notebook or typing on an old fashioned typewriter, but the only real advantage of these methods is so writers can try to make themselves interesting at parties by saying stuff like, "I do all my writing in longhand, it's so much more organic that way," or impressing hipsters by saying, "I prefer using typewriters when I write, but I'll only use an old manual typewriter if it's vintage."

But typewriters and moleskin notebooks are ultimately besides the point because you're a writer and nobody is going to invite you to a party anyway, so a computer is a better and more practical way to go.

It's also good to keep in mind that the last guy using a typewriter who had any kind of impact as a writer was Ted Kaczynski, and he lacked any follow-up to his initial fame. But he did come up with a memorable moniker — The Unabomber — so at least he understood the importance of branding.

CHAPTER FIFTEEN

The world is filled with no-talents and hacks and some of them make a good living writing completely unoriginal and unimaginative screenplays. But these professionals don't have a monopoly on unoriginality. All kinds of people from all walks of life are unimaginative, but they just don't have the imagination to realize this. The averageness that is within you, that has guided you through all the mundane and insignificant moments of your life, is a potential gold mine waiting to be tapped. And the fact that I just used a tired and cliched gold mine metaphor to express this point is proof that I don't just talk the talk, I walk the walk!

The most important element in any dramatic work is conflict. And there is no better film to study as an example of great dramatic conflict than the MST3K-riffed movie, *Racket Girls*. You could, if you wanted to, make the argument that there are better examples, like for instance, every other film ever made, including ATM security camera footage, but for the purposes of this book, *Racket Girls* is perfect, because what more compelling form of conflict is there than female wrestling? Think of how much better most Meryl Streep movies would be if there was female wrestling in them. I honestly don't see how *The Hours*, for instance, would have been hurt by the inclusion of not just Female Wrestling, but the Tour de France of Female Wrestling -- Female Mud Wrestling. As it is, the movie more than lived up to its poster copy. "If You Kill Yourself After Seeing One Film This Year, Make It The Hours," so a little girl-on-girl action would have been an improvement, but granted, you can say that about almost anything involving Virginia Wolf.

(If my disparaging remarks about *The Hours* are upsetting to you, that's too bad. I'm not one of those writers who is too timid to take on films released twenty years ago that aren't talked about that often anymore. Sorry, but I call them as I used to see them.)

There is wrestling but no mud or nudity in *Racket Girls* because it wasn't until taboos broke down in the late 1960s that women were finally allowed to be explicitly degraded by men in cinema.

Racket Girls was ahead of its time and maybe now we've finally reached the point where audiences might be ready for it, but unfortunately, this means they would have to watch it. This could be the year that *Racket Girls* gets a critical reassessment, but don't hold your breath (unless you want to enhance your orgasm).

If you are a forward-thinking visionary, you're in for a hard time as a writer. The phrase, "he was ahead of his time" is usually heard at paupers funerals to bemoan that such and such a person didn't make a dime in his or her lifetime. Vincent Van Gogh, who only sold one painting while he was alive, could talk your ear off about the hazards of being ahead of your time.

But if you are a writer of cheesy movies, being ahead of your time is not going to be a problem. Your natural tendency will be to stay several paces behind whatever it is that's going on in the world. Your job is to keep your eye out for what's in the zeitgeist, and then cash in on whatever trends happen to be zeiting and/or geisting. And don't think that this cynical thought is exclusive to a cheesy screenwriting guide, several books that claim to promote good writing have advocated this very notion.

Writer's agents are always telling their clients to be "marketable." From a practical standpoint, this is good advice, and to be honest, I'm not the best person to emulate on this topic. When you've made as many Joe Besser references as I have, you kind of lose any credibility you might have had as a modern marketing guru.

I have been known to have my finger on the pulse of the zeitgeist; unfortunately it's usually the zeitgeist of 1945.

So I will admit that during my years in Hollywood, I was a little bit, shall we say, out of touch. When my agent sent me to MTV Films to pitch a movie meant for the youth market, I proposed a *Barnaby Jones* reboot (and the fact that I'm still making *Barnaby Jones* references all these years later is proof that I haven't learned much).

And when MTV was looking for a hip and edgy reality show, the Pimp My Prostate premise I came up with was dismissed out of hand. even though the security guard who was called in to escort me off the studio lot thought the idea had real merit.

But this is the world of television I'm talking about, and it mostly doesn't apply to what this book is about, so please don't let my career failures prevent you from hanging on my every word of wisdom about succeeding in Hollywood.

CHAPTER SIXTEEN

When you are writing your script, you have start on page one. You could start on page twenty-five; it would certainly make pages one through twenty-four much easier to read. Unfortunately, people who read and evaluate screenplays for a living tend to look askance at a script that begins with 24 blank pages. This makes it difficult for them to envision what your script will look like when it is filmed. And looking at blank, empty space reminds them a little too much of their own lives. Plus, if someone else has already sent them a script of blank pages, they're going to think you stole that person's idea and they won't have the same respect for you that they had for the first writer who sent them 24 blank pages.

So start on page one. Start with something that will really grab a reader's attention. The Joe Eszterhaus screenplay for *Showgirls* sold for $3 million. That comes to almost one dollar for every brain cell destroyed while reading the script, so it is was an impressive sale.

Here is the attention-grabbing first page of *Showgirls*. Note how it brings you deep into the world of the story right off the bat.

FADE IN:

EXT. LAS VEGAS. DAY.

Pussy, pussy,

pussy, pussy, pussy, pussy, pussy, pussy, pussy, pussy, pussy, pussy, pussy,
pussy, pussy, pussy, pussy, pussy, pussy, pussy, pussy, pussy, pussy, pussy,
pussy, pussy, pussy, pussy, pussy, pussy, pussy, pussy, pussy, pussy, pussy,
pussy, pussy, pussy, pussy, pussy, pussy, pussy, pussy, pussy, pussy, pussy,
pussy, pussy, pussy, pussy, pussy, pussy, pussy, pussy, pussy, pussy, pussy,
pussy, pussy, pussy, pussy, pussy, pussy, pussy, pussy, pussy, pussy, pussy,
pussy, pussy, pussy, pussy, pussy, pussy, pussy, pussy, pussy, pussy, pussy,
pussy, pussy, pussy, pussy, pussy, pussy, pussy, pussy, pussy, pussy, pussy,
pussy, pussy, pussy, pussy, pussy, pussy, pussy, pussy, pussy, pussy, pussy,
pussy, pussy, pussy, pussy, pussy, pussy, pussy, pussy, pussy, pussy, pussy,
pussy, pussy, pussy, pussy, pussy, pussy, pussy, pussy, pussy, pussy, pussy,
pussy, pussy, pussy, pussy, pussy, pussy, pussy, pussy, pussy, pussy, pussy,
pussy, pussy, pussy, pussy, pussy, pussy, pussy, pussy, pussy, pussy, pussy,
pussy, pussy, pussy, pussy, pussy, pussy, pussy, pussy, pussy, pussy, pussy,
pussy, pussy, pussy, pussy, pussy, pussy, pussy, pussy, pussy, pussy, pussy,
pussy, pussy, pussy, pussy, pussy, pussy, pussy, pussy, pussy, pussy, pussy,
pussy, pussy, pussy, pussy, pussy, pussy, pussy, pussy, pussy, pussy, pussy,
pussy, pussy, pussy, pussy, pussy, pussy, pussy, pussy, pussy, pussy, pussy,
pussy, pussy, pussy, pussy, pussy, pussy, pussy, pussy, pussy, pussy.

See? It's exactly the film you ended up watching on the big screen. You can envision the whole movie. When Hollywood executives read it, they couldn't write Joe Eszterhaus a $3 million check fast enough. The movie was made immediately and the result was a cinematic experience that has scarred souls the world over. Films like *Showgirls* are why the "clear history" tab was invented. It was the first motion picture that made the producers of snuff films feel comparatively good about that they did for a living. Yes, the legacy of *Showgirls* is a rich and lasting one, it will continue to make people feel empty and bereft for decades to come.

And it all started with that first page.

But great ideas like *Showgirls* come along only once every five minutes or so; you can't just assume you're going to be struck with that kind of inspiration.

So put a lot of thought and effort into your first page. It's an intimidating process that will seem overwhelming to you, but remember, if you keep writing and don't give up, what you are working on could one day be a major motion picture that broken men masturbate to.

CHAPTER SEVENTEEN

If you are at the point where you have already written an incoherent outline that is going to be of no help to you, and if you have no idea what your story is, who the characters are, or what any of it is supposed to mean, then you are on the right track towards a cheesy triumph. But you still have to figure out how to move your story forward even while it's not going anywhere.

Let's face it, the whole writing-a-screenplay thing is a huge pain in the ass. It's a specialized field that just a few people are good at, which is why each year only about half the population of the earth ever attempt to write one.

If you don't want to go through the hassle of writing a full length movie where nothing takes place, you could always just write a short film where nothing takes place within a tighter time frame. There's a lot to be said for this option, because once your short film is made, you can enter it into film festivals, and this can lead to a glamorous life of flying to national and international film competitions at your own expense with no possible financial payoff. But as appealing as this sounds, maybe you should stick to feature films. They are harder to write, but there is at least a possible pot to piss in at the end of the rainbow.

And once you do embark on the writing of a full length cheesy movie, I would recommend you make sure the pages of your script come in chronological order. There might be something to be said for throwing your screenplay into the air, letting it land all over the place, and then collating the pages randomly. If your plot already doesn't make any sense, this could possibly improve the quality of your story.

For instance, if the order of the scenes in the MST3K-riffed film *Monster-A-Go-Go* had been thoughtlessly rearranged, it would have only made the film better, although what really helps the flow of action in that story is not watching it at all. In other words, not writing *Monster-A-Go-Go* and not filming *Monster-A-Go-Go* would have meant a vastly superior *Monster-A-Go-Go*.

But often these kinds of improvements don't occur to a writer as he or she is writing a script. Sometimes the best way to tighten your story and more sharply define your characters is to abandon your screenplay outright and see if they're hiring at Wal-Mart, but finishing what you started will ultimately be a much more satisfying experience for you, if not for the general public.

There was one instance of a movie where they messed up the pages and filmed it in the wrong order, but *Memento* is a unique case. It launched Christopher Nolan to a life of wealth and acclaim, but oddly enough, my obsessive jealousy of him has occurred in a straightforward, linear fashion.

Just remember, if your pointless, rambling, incoherent screenplay doesn't have a beginning, middle and end, people will have a hard time following it.

CHAPTER EIGHTEEN

Padding is one of the most important, if not the most important element in the writing of a cheesy MST3K-worthy screenplay. And there are practical reasons for padding out a screenplay that go beyond artistic considerations. Movies are contractually required by movie theater chains to be a certain length. This has been the case for much of film history. Only in the first decade of the twentieth century, when the main movie-going experience consisted of watching one minute strips of film on a Nickelodeon machine, were screenwriters not required to write feature-length films. Your film could be as short as one minute, and you didn't have to write dialogue. It was a golden age for lazy-ass writers. The guy who had to do the most work was the dude in charge of composing the old timey music that provided live accompaniment for the film, and lucky for him, there was a real vogue for old timey music back in the old timey era.

When you can't think of anything to happen in your cheesy script, but you need to keep things going anyway, padding is the answer. The reason for this is that studio executives, producers, and audiences have unreasonable expectations when it comes to movies. As a story unfolds in a screenplay, they expect shit to happen. And who is it that has to bear the brunt of this dickish demand? Screenwriters. They are the ones who have to come up with stuff for actors to say and do, and even when the actors improvise, they like to have a script that they can wipe their asses with beforehand as a warm up exercise. So no matter what, there has to be a screenplay, and like it or not, the task of writing a screenplay usually falls upon the screenwriter.

That is why padding is so essential to the art of cheesy screenwriting. If it weren't for padding, only screenwriters who are capable of screenwriting would be allowed to write screenplays, and that is an unsustainable system that no one wants to live with.

The sad truth is that there is prejudice and discrimination in the movie business. In many cases, writers are blocked from working on prestige projects only because they have no talent for writing.

But they do have a talent for padding, while some of America's most revered filmmakers have no padding skills at all. For instance, if Francis Ford Coppola and Mario Puzo had any knack for the art of the pad, there would have been a long scene of Don Corleone and Fredo driving to the fruit and vegetable stand where *The Godfather* is gunned down. Sure, many would argue that the moment when the gunfire starts is the exciting part, and they are right, which is exactly why it isn't padding. But a half hour scene of them driving to the exciting part: now, that's padding! And if the exciting part never even happens, that adds the important element of pointlessness, thus bringing padding to the next level.

The scene where Michael Corleone shoots Sollozzo and Chief McCluski is a suspenseful, riveting scene, one of the most memorable in film history. But in the sequence immediately preceding it, they drive all the way from midtown Manhattan to New Jersey and then to the Bronx. We only see them for a few moments in the car, and that scene is quite suspenseful in itself, but think of what a missed opportunity for padding it was! A drive from midtown to Jersey to the Bronx could have taken up most of the movie. Coppola and Puzo could have easily filled up pages and pages of padding, then knocked off early and relaxed over a plate of pasta and a carafe of Coppola vineyard vino, with maybe a glass or two of vintage Smothers Brothers merlot to wash it all down.

(Have you finished googling the Smothers Brothers and learned that they have a wine vineyard? Good, we can move on.)

But instead of swigging wine, Coppola and Puzo decided to figure out how to execute a couple of sequences that redefined what drama and suspense can be in a major motion picture. And all they have to show for all that hard work are a few Oscars and millions of dollars. What were they thinking?

Sure, I'm making it seem like avoiding padding was good for *The Godfather*, and in some ways it was, but most screenwriters aren't even capable of writing *Godfather, Part III*, much less *Godfathers I & II*. Most cheesy screenwriters aim a little lower, like maybe *Troll II*, a cheesy movie that was made despite there being no *Troll I*. And *Troll II* is so bad that even though it's a sequel to a movie that doesn't exist, it is still not as good as the original.

It's all very well and good to make your script more exciting by tightening the action and upping the entertainment value, but some cheesy scribes don't live in the world of well and good, so those people had better pad the fuck out of their screenplays. The technique and craft that go into the making of a movie like *The Godfather* are of no concern to a writer of cheesy movies. A good rule of thumb is — leave the gun, take the contrivance.

To really understand the art of padding, you need go no further than the MST3K padsterpiece, *Lost Continent*.

This movie is an example of filmmakers dreaming big while aiming low. The producer of this opus, Robert Lippert, made a movie that has stood the test of time — film lovers ignore and neglect it every bit as much today as when it first opened in 1955.

In case you've forgotten *Lost Continent* (and if you haven't, please consult a doctor, you may be suffering from a severe lack of memory loss), it is a film that features a lot of Rock Climbing. Lots and lots of Rock Climbing. This is an aspect of the film that we couldn't help but mention on Mystery Science Theater 3000, because not mentioning Rock Climbing in conjunction with *Lost Continent* is like not mentioning Lou Gehrig's Disease in conjunction with *Pride of the Yankees*. (The fact that Lou Gehrig contracted Lou Gehrig's Disease is proof that even classic Hollywood movies are not above inserting implausible coincidences into their plots.)

In *Lost Continent*, the padding was throughly integrated into the film to the point where it was hard to tell where the padding began and the storytelling ended. It was even more difficult to figure out where the storytelling started; the only thing we know for sure is that the words "The End" did eventually appear on the screen, and most film scholars agree this was the most satisfying part of the movie.

In *Lost Continent,* the main characters have to climb up a bunch of rocks in order to see all the stock footage that's waiting for them at the top of the mountain. Therefore they have to climb and climb and climb and climb and climb. And the director filmed every moment of it. A more conventional filmmaker might have had a montage or a jump-cut to show the passage of time. The exciting part happens when the the tiny lizards start fighting in front of even tinier model sets, so why not get to this stuff as quickly as possible?

Because then you'd just have to pad out the stuff that comes after it, so what's the point? Well, here's the point I will make: it's never too soon to get to the padding. If you are going to write a cheesy MST3K-worthy script, don't delay the padding. Padding is your friend, through bad times and worse times, slow times and slower times.

I really can't emphasize enough how great padding is. The padding in *Lost Continent* was amazing, and quite admirable in the way the padding was used to pad out the film. The way the filmmakers took the rock climbing scene and just padded and padded and padded and padded and padded and padded and padded and padded and padded and padded and padded and padded and padded and padded and padded and padded and padded and padded was impressive. It was a great example of how not just a film, but a play, or a TV show, or even a book, can be lengthened just by repeating something over and over and over and over and over and over and over and over and over again.

Repetition is the cheesy screenwriter's best friend, or, perhaps more accurately, it's the dull friend that overstays its welcome and never leaves, but nevertheless it is a good friend because when all the other tools of the trade have left you, repetition will stick around and be the same thing it's always been for you. It can't be repeated often enough, repetition is the cheesy screenwriter's friend. It is. It really is. It really, really, really is. Seriously, what I just said about repetition is true. So very, very, very, very true. It can't be stated enough, although I probably just have. The only thing that could stop me from rhapsodizing over and over again about the greatness of repetition and padding is that I may be about to get called up on assault and battery charges for beating a joke to death.

CHAPTER NINETEEN

It has been said that the best kind of writing is autobiographical. This applies to bad writing as well. If you want to write a cheesy script where absolutely nothing happens, if will help if you've had experience in life not doing anything. Have you recently gone for a long walk that was completely uneventful? Well, try to incorporate that event into your own writing, and don't stint on the details. Have you sat in one dull place for hours, to the point where you were wondering if being bored to death is covered by Obamacare? Have you had an endless conversation with a coworker who is every bit as much of a dullard as you are? Get that all into you writing, leave nothing out!

And try not to be disheartened if your life isn't as mundane and devoid of purpose as you'd like it to be. Every living person, even you, is capable of lacking imagination. Just because you've never actually sat and watched paint dry doesn't mean you can't capture the essence of what that feels like in your screenplay.

Dare to dream the dreams of the dull.

But do you have the guts to be cheesy? It is the purpose of every artist to touch another person's life, and if you write a cheesy screenplay in just the right way, you could actually waste the time of someone you've never even met. That's right, you have it within you to steal precious moments from the lives of total strangers. If your cheesy screenplay is produced and made into a cheesy movie, people in other states, even other countries, are going to be bored out of their skulls and you'll be the one who made it happen.

That is why it is important to jot down all the uneventful, insignificant things that happen to you. Your small, sheltered life has made you brain-dead and oblivious to the world around you. So write what you know.

Still, maybe you don't have what it takes to fill up those blank spaces with blank words. You might end up having to face the harsh truth that you have talent. It's just possible that when you sit down to write, a million great ideas will gush forth, and the application of your intelligence, combined with a comprehension of craft, will result in an entertaining and fast-paced script. I'm not saying that this will necessarily happen to you, but if you do find yourself afflicted with inspiration, don't panic. Stay calm, count to three, and hopefully the lightbulb that went off above your head will turn out to be just a flash of bird shit.

Talent can be a hard thing for some people to face, but you have to be brutally honest with yourself. If you are too brilliant to write the next Manos: The Hands of Fate, accept it and learn to live with it. Some people just don't have the skills to be incompetent.

CHAPTER TWENTY

The importance of preparation should be obvious to anyone who knows anything about writing, as is the importance of something else, which I can't remember right now because this chapter is pretty much off the cuff, but I think I remember hearing somewhere that outlines are great because they give you a roadmap to your story. It's like a GPS system that you install in your screenplay before you've even gotten started, except it doesn't have a built-in voice, which is fortunate, because in my case, that voice would be constantly saying, "recalibrating."

Another thing that writers do is make notes as they are working on their script. It's a way to keep a dialogue with yourself as you write. For instance, here is a note the writer of *Castle of Fu Manchu* made to himself as he was writing:

"Acjenfnfhfjsjdncywiqmsnchfhehejsjsndjdjggsbsjsppwjdnxjjdjwjaksjdjeg-gajsiwos."

If you've seen *Castle of Fu Manchu*, you probably remember that this is exactly the kind of thinking that ended up in the finished product.

As you might imagine, the script for *Batman v. Superman* posed many challenges. Keeping a set of notes helped the writer of that film come up with the solution to that movie's third act. Here is an excerpt:

"For Christ's sake, in just about every scene so far, I've had Bruce Wayne/Batman say that Superman is the biggest threat to humanity in the history of the world and must be destroyed, so now how the hell am I supposed to team them up? Maybe there's something in their collective past that can unite them, something from their family history... wait a minute, I think I've got it! Bruce Wayne's mother's name is Martha, and Clark Kent's mother is also named Martha! That's it! That... Wait, who am I kidding? That's the worst idea ever. Back to the drawing board..."

Later that day, the *Batman v. Superman* writer made this note:

"Fuck, I still can't think of anything. I'm just gonna go with the Martha/Martha thing..."

So, as you can see, by going through the note-writing process, the writer was better able to realize he was running on empty and then just had to go with whatever his most recent idea happened to be. The lesson to be learned from this is that when you are writing your script, pray that two of your character's mothers have the same name, otherwise you're screwed.

But it's not just complex ideas that benefit from notes to yourself, simple ideas have their place as well. Here's a note the writer of the latest Fast and Furious movie made just as he was beginning to write the script:

"It occurs to me that what this story needs is lots of car chases. I think I'm gonna go with that. I hope the producers are cool with this."

See? They say that writing is 1% inspiration and 99% perspiration, and that is certainly the case with cheesy movies, because if there's one undeniable fact about perspiration, it's that it stinks.

CHAPTER TWENTY-ONE

If I've disparaged the writers of Superhero and Fast and Furious movies, it's for a solid reason based in cinema aesthetics - I'm viciously jealous of them. But I will give them some props: they are tasked with writing movies that are not just cheesy, but long. There is no denying that cheesy screenwriters from the era of films that *Mystery Science Theater 3000* riffed had it easier than today's cheesy screenwriters, because the running time of most of the MST3K-era films were at most 75 minutes, in some cases just an hour. Under these circumstances, sucking was far less time consuming.

But in any era, there is a difference between a hack writer and a professional hack writer. Being a pro requires a great deal of effort. You may have watched the scene in *The Shining* where Jack Nicholson writes "All work and no play makes Jack a dull boy" over and over again for weeks on end. But don't forget, this is a character in a fictional story. It's not real life. Being able to sustain a work of prose with that level of consistency is something you only see in the movies. And multitasking is not something that comes easily to most writers, so if you think you can focus on completing a piece of writing and also find time to ax-murder Scatman Crothers, you are deluding yourself. But that's okay; self-delusion is an essential component of any writer's life.

This is true of all writers, and all artists, good or bad. Pursuing a career that involves creative expression is a fool's errand, but being foolish is a lifestyle choice that offers many rewards if you can endure the periods of bitter disappointment and crushing failure that are like push notifications from a cruel and indifferent universe.

There is a surefire way to avoid failure: don't attempt anything creative and just go about your life in a normal, conventional way. In my case, during my lifetime, when they are looking for fools to go on errands, I have always raised my hand to volunteer, and I have never regretted it, except for all those times I thought I regretted it, but that was my fear talking, and when my fear speaks, it is in THX Dolby surround-sound stereo. My psyche is wired for fear the way state of the art movie theaters are wired for sound. It's amazing the special effects my insecurity manages to achieve on such a limited budget.

The specter of failure hangs over a creative person at all times. It causes a dark and gloomy climate, but these are the moments in your life when you need to be a climate denier. Remember, all of your fear, all of your insecurity, and all of your self-doubt is just like global warming — almost entirely man-made.

CHAPTER TWENTY-TWO

Have you ever watched a movie where you couldn't follow the plot and had no idea what was going on? When I worked at *Mystery Science Theater 3000*, it was my job to be confused by filmmaking on a daily basis, whereas many of you have had to pay money for the honor of watching a movie and not knowing what the hell is happening. Either way, most completely incoherent films are the result of meticulous planning. But you can't cover everything in the outline. The over-complicated story developments and entertainment-extracting dialogue scenes are often inserted as the screenplay is developed. So go ahead and write an intricate outline, but leave room for any off the top-of-your-head, spur-of-the-moment ideas you might happen to come up with. That spontaneous brain-fart might turn out to be a million dollar idea, especially if the guy you stole it from sues you for a million dollars.

The good thing about baffling plot points is they leave room for scene after scene of characters having endless conversations with each other that are supposed to explain what happened in a previous scene while setting up what will happen in a subsequent scene in a way that makes the current scene completely unbearable.

But despite all I'm saying, do not feel shame about being a cheesy screenwriter. Cheesy screenwriting has many societal advantages - it provides growth and job opportunities for people who work in fields other than motion pictures. Video arcades, board games, amusement parks, bowling alleys, massage parlors, and countless other industries are the beneficiaries of cheesy screenwriting, because cheesy movies tend to encourage people to patronize other businesses. Your attempts at screenwriting are an investment in the future of America. Your capacity to bore is the lifeblood of our nation.

And there's a good way to find out just how boring your screenplay is before you send it out into the world: hold a reading of your script. A bunch of actors sit around a table and read from your screenplay, with different performers reading different parts. This is very helpful to a good screenplay. It can show its author what's working in a script and what needs to be changed. It is even more helpful when it comes to cheesy screenplays. If everyone reading from the script is yawning and passing out from your finely crafted tedium, you'll know your script is everything a cheesy movie is supposed to be. You can feel proud that you've managed to translate the natural dullness of your everyday life into a whole different medium.

One thing that often happens after the reading of a script is a feedback session where everyone who has attended can give you notes and evaluate your writing. This sounds intimidating, but you should listen to all critiques with an open mind, and hear what everyone has to say before you react with a sullen, resentful dismissal of all who dare criticize your work.

The most useful way to deal with criticism is to assume that the person giving it does not have your best interests at heart. Often, they are also writers and they want to succeed even more than you do. Their so-called "constructive" criticism will be passive/aggressive at best.

They will say things like:

"I think the first act needs work, but at least the second act is worse."

"Your script seems as personal to you as my mom's cancer was to me."

"This is exactly what William Goldman would have written if he had no talent."

But you must allow others tell you what they think about your work. While they are giving you their carefully considered assessment of your script, put both hands over your ears and repeatedly say, "LA LA LA, I CAN'T HEAR YOU, LA LA LA, I CAN'T HEAR YOU!" This kind of back-and-forth, give-and-take will make it a two-way conversation.

No one can write a screenplay in a vacuum. For one thing, you'd have to be really, really small, and even then, it'd be kind of cramped and dirty. But my point is that the opinions of others can be quite valuable, even, and maybe especially, when they are negative.

This might sound arrogant, but in my case I have found that I am perfectly capable of feeling defeated and demoralized without the help of anyone else, thank you very much.

I probably have no business disparaging cheesy movies that are confusing. And who am I to bitch about not following the plot? Life confuses me and I can never follow the plot of daily existence. It sometimes seems to me that other people have picked up on the linear narrative that is happening all around us, but I tend to always wander in late, several steps behind, not quite sure what's going on. I mean, when you come right down to it, where do I get off making fun of cheesy movies, when I spent my young adulthood — the 1970s to be exact — abusing drugs and living my life as if I was the star of a juvenile delinquent B-movie with some of the dullest delinquency of all time. If my existence in those days had been a screenplay, it would have been rejected for having less action and energy than *Manos: The Hands Of Fate*.

And then what happened in the third act of this part of my life? I went to rehab and sobered up, just like what would happen in any number of cliched After-School Specials. All these years later I am still sober and alive and it is just so hackneyed. I wouldn't be surprised if the universe is riffing my every move. But regardless, I just keep moving forward, flailing about as I try do my best, even if, to God, I'm Torgo.

CHAPTER TWENTY-THREE

Let's take a moment to acknowledge how daunting it is to write an entire screenplay based on nothing more than your own imagination. It's like trying to drive a car with no gas, and yes, you are right, I don't have the imagination to come up with a better metaphor than the done-a-million times empty gas tank one. It is a cliche, and cliches upset me so much that when I come across one, I'm like a deer in the headlights.

At certain times during the writing of your screenplay, you will be tempted to give up. For me, that point usually comes right after I've typed, "Fade In." But don't give up. I think you'll find that at just the moment when you are ready to click "delete file," you will suddenly type in some gibberish that makes no sense to you or anyone else and at that moment you will be one shitty idea closer to an entire cheesy movie.

And it might be unlike anything anyone has ever done, or, more likely, a rip-off of something someone else did that was unlike anything anyone has ever done. But I would never encourage anyone to rip-off a popular TV show or movie. It's much more sensible to rip-off an unpopular TV show or movie. If you steal the premise of *Game of Thrones*, federal prosecutors will be on to you in an instant. But if you steal the premise of *I'm Dickens, He's Fenster,* there's a good chance you're going to make a clean getaway.

Okay, are you back from googling *I'm Dickens, He's Fenster?* Good, let's continue.

The world needs good writers now more than ever, but luckily, Hollywood is often out of touch with what the world needs. Writers who can't write are often blessed with skills that writers who can write are lacking: stepping on people's toes, stabbing folks in the back, using others to get ahead, sucker punching a rival. It's odd that so many writers have no aptitude for athletics when you consider that show business is frequently a contact sport.

Writing is thought to be a lonely, solitary profession. But writing isn't only about you and your writing. It's about how you interact with the industry professionals you have to undermine and manipulate so that your cheesy screenplay can see the light of day.

Some have been known to seek career advancement by sleeping their way to the top. But forget about that. You're a writer, nobody want's to sleep with you. And if you're a writer of cheesy MST3K-style films, the word sleeping only applies to the state your films will be putting audiences in. But don't loose sleep over this. If you become successful enough, you can pay someone to sleep with you. Of course, many find the very idea of having sex with a prostitute repugnant, but there are documented cases of hookers who are willing to have sex with screenwriters.

If you really have what it takes, you will not surrender your dream. Giving up on the cheesy script you're working on requires a common sense that any true writer, good or bad, is just not capable of. The act of even writing a screenplay is proof that being sensible is not a priority to you. Even writers who are great artists and who express the truthful nature of life in their work wouldn't be able to write in the first place if they didn't have a certain detachment from reality, or at least reality as it's presented to them by other people.

The act of writing can be quite frustrating in the early stages. If you don't believe me, look at the original titles of some of these famous titles:

WINNIE THE FUCKING POO

ARE YOU THERE, GOD? IT'S ME MARGARET, AND I'M NEVER GOING TO FINISH THIS GODDAMN BOOK!

TO KILL A MOCKINGBIRD, WHO WON'T SHUT UP AND LET ME CONCENTRATE ON THIS PIECE OF SHIT BOOK!

I, ROBOT, SUCK AT THIS

THE BOY WHO LIKED TO JERK-OFF INTO LAMB CHOPS

Actually, the work on that last book was going well; Philip Roth just arbitrarily decided to change the title to *Portnoy's Complaint* at a later date.

Writing is an arduous journey with an uncertain outcome. Only a crazy person would attempt it. Which is not to say that I'm comparing writers to crazy people like serial killers. Unlike writers, serial killers are willing to leave their rooms and go out and meet new people. And they have a much easier time attracting the interest of agents.

I should probably point out that not all writers are the awkward anti-social borderline catatonics I'm portraying them to be. Just because I am an awkward anti-social borderline catatonic, that doesn't mean I should project that on all writers. It's just that the idea that lots of other people are as fucked up as I am has always given me great comfort.

There is a commonality among all in the human race. But what unites us and makes us feel like we are all just like each other is the knowledge that everyone else has insecurities, anxieties, hang-ups and neurosis, too. We can feel better about ourselves knowing that others feel bad about themselves as well. The understanding that so many people on the planet are lonely makes us feel less alone.

CHAPTER TWENTY-FOUR

So you've kept your personal demons at bay long enough to hack out an outline. After much mental masturbation (or as I like to call it, masturbation), you've written your first ten pages. What's next? Hate to tell you this, but now you have to get to your first plot point.

What is a plot point? There are lots of examples from films that would give you a good example, but instead let's go with *Manos: The Hands of Fate.*

The first plot point in Manos comes after they've been driving the car for a while and they get out of the car. This announces to the audience that they have arrived at the spot where most of the action will take place. This is a bit misleading since there's not going to be any action, but withholding information from audiences can be an effective tool, and at this point Manos is unsuccessfully withholding the information that absolutely nothing is going to happen for the rest of the movie.

This information might upset certain audience members if most of them hadn't already fallen asleep at this point. That's the beauty of cheesy screenwriting — if you can put viewers to sleep soon enough, you don't have to worry about putting them to sleep later on, and as a writer, your main concern about your audience will be to try not to wake them.

But succeeding at this is not as easy as it sounds. You can't pull the wool over an audience's eyes if those eyes are already covered with sleep masks. Some writers are only cheesy enough to make the audience drowsy while others are in danger of being arrested as barbiturate dealers if they try to smuggle their scripts across state lines. The rapid eye movement that happens during the sleep that writers of cheesy movies induce is the only kind of rapid movement that is ever associated with their films.

But I still haven't explained to you what a plot point is yet, have I? Put simply, a plot point is that moment in a movie when something happens, so needless to say, there are hardly any examples from MST3K-riffed films that I can point to.

Isn't art supposed to reflect life? You may be wondering why I'm bringing up the subject of art while discussing cheesy movies riffed on *Mystery Science Theater 3000*, but please hear me out. I'm just saying that most of the MST3K-riffed films might be boring, but life is boring, so these films reflect life. If that's the case then why can't they be considered art? This may seem like a stretch, but please consider my point and try not to dismiss it out of hand just because it's stupid.

It's actually a little weird that we often interpret life as mundane and boring. By all scientific accounts, life is an amazing spectacle. The planet we live on, as damaged as it is, is a constantly evolving biological and geological wonder. Yet we frequently treat life as if it's a marathon showing of *Plan 9 From Outer Space* that we're forced to watch.

The truth is that we want art to be better than life. Mostly we want movies to be an escape from life. The miracle that is all around us is something we want filmed entertainment to relieve us from.

So who are any us to judge Ed Wood when we already think God is a hack?

CHAPTER TWENTY-FIVE

Every screenplay needs an inciting incident. It's the moment in a script where something happens that affects the rest of the movie. In *Gone With The Wind*, it's the moment when the Civil War starts and all the plantation-owning traitors who engage in human trafficking realize that the brutal human enslavement that is so precious to their elegant way of life is being threatened. There are many moments that made *Gone With The Wind* one of the most beloved racist films of all time, but without the inciting incident, none of the subsequent romancing of slavery would have been possible.

Gone With The Wind is one of the most prestigious and honored films of all time. It presents bigotry, as well as marital rape, in a positive light. But in all likelihood the cheesy movie that you are working on will be low budget, so don't even try writing a movie as high-minded as *Gone With The Wind*.

In *Forrest Gump*, the inciting incident was the main character being born an idiot. This led to adventures that resulted in him being a millionaire with a hot girlfriend. A complete moron attaining massive wealth is the essence of the American Dream. Audiences will always relate to an imbecile with a good heart, so it's better to make the hero of your movie an idiot rather than a genius. Brilliant people are often the bad guys in movies. Think of every James Bond villain. They are called masterminds for a reason. And they like cats, but that's besides the point. They are geniuses, so American audiences root against them.

Villainous henchmen, on the other hand, are allowed to be dumb, but that subject hits a little close to home for this author, so I will move on.

It's been pointed out by others that the main characters in horror films are almost always idiots. They run into dark wooded areas and ignore the sign that says, "Caution: The Ax-Wielding Psycho Is Obviously Lurking Right Here, You Fucking Moron." They walk into empty houses while nervously crying out, "Guys? Guys? This isn't funny!" when it's obvious that in a tense moment like this, the last thing anyone wants is comedy criticism.

But audiences not only root for these idiots, they relate to them, because by purchasing a ticket to watch the film, they engaged in something similarly idiotic.

You might present Sherlock Holmes as a counter-argument. He is what people in Boston would call wicked smart. But I won't entertain that argument because it doesn't support my thesis.

But inciting incidents, whether they involve smart or dumb characters, incite the incidents in all films. Godzilla movies always have the exact same inciting incident - a shit load of radiation turns a lizard into a mutant monster. You might think the part where Godzilla destroys an entire city is the most important part of a Godzilla film, but if it hadn't been for that radiation, he'd still just be a tiny little lizard, and if you saw a film where millions of people are killed by a pet store lizard, it would strain credibility, but a giant mutant monster killing millions is at least realistic.

Post-World War II anxiety about fallout from nuclear radiation is what initially inspired Japanese film studio Toho to make Godzilla movies. The atomic destruction of Hiroshima and Nagasaki were the inciting incidents that incited the inciting incidents in all Godzilla stories. This is good news for aspiring screenwriters in the modern age. We are more in danger of an apocalypse than ever, so there is lots of potential real-life inspiration out there, and if a brand new mutant monster emerges from the rubble, maybe you can be the first to write a screenplay about him or her, but you'll only be able to use existing technology, so it's probably more accurate to say that maybe you'll be the first to turn their stories into a cave painting.

On the other hand, if you are among the billions killed in a global catastrophe, it could hamper your ability to write your film and for audiences to come see it. I'm afraid that when it comes the end of the world, the glass is a bit on the half-empty side.

The *Mad Max Fury Road* inciting incident is happening right now as we speak. People in power are ruining the planet and destroying our natural resources, so cheesy screenwriters, don't let this opportunity to write a dystopian blockbuster pass you by, although if you do sell your script, make sure you get paid in gasoline and water.

CHAPTER TWENTY-SIX

Generally, screenplays are broken up into three acts. In the first act, some shit happens. In the second act, some more shit happens. And in the third act, all the shit that was supposed to happen, happened already, so the movie ends arbitrarily. I'm sorry if this was too technical, but I couldn't quite figure out how to put it in layman's terms.

Recent movies from the Marvel Universe have previews of the sequels during the end credits. But it would probably be a bit presumptuous of you to start writing the end credit preview scenes into your script. Also, since it will be years before your movie is made, if it's made at all, there is no point in writing the closing credits into your screenplay. You have no idea who the key grip or the catering service is going to be, so it will all just be guessing. Not to pat myself on the back, but I believe I am the first screenwriting instructor ever to make the point that you shouldn't write spec-closing credits in your screenplay. You're welcome.

While most movies may have a three act structure, the way that structure is executed varies from film to film. In the case of *Batman v. Superman: Dawn of Justice,* the first act ended at least two hours after most other films had let out and the audience went home. That movie was so long, many couples who went to see it on a first date celebrated their silver anniversary as they exited the theater. Some audience members couldn't tweet about what they thought of the film because by the time it was over, the software on their phones was not compatible with the mobile network they were using. Even people who liked the film regretted that they never had the chance to watch their children grow up. It was a long movie is what I'm trying to say.

But *Batman v. Superman* does not apply to you because only a professional screenwriter is considered skillful enough to write a bloated overlong soul-killing cinematic slog like BvS. These kinds of movies cost a lot of money to make so they are not going to hire some novice to write them when they can get someone just as bad at twice the salary.

Sometimes a three act structure cannot be gauged by what the writer does. The structure of certain films are determined more by the behavior of the person watching it. For instance, studies have revealed that the five minute mark is the spot in the MST3K-riffed film *Fire Maidens From Outer Space* when most viewers contemplate gauging their eyes out. The twenty minute mark is when blood starts spurting out of their ears. At the sixty minute mark they become drooling idiots. That's the point where they are actually capable of enjoying the movie but by then it's almost over.

You know how a great movie will stay with you for years afterwards? The after-effects of a cheesy movie can be just as long-lasting. The lobotomized state that a movie like *Fire Maidens From Outer Space* puts you in is something you may never recover from. Sure, you'll walk around as if everything is normal, but your friends and family will know that something is wrong, deeply wrong.

When a movie is really bad — Manos bad — the first act can be the point where you contemplate harming yourself, the second act is where you decide to harm yourself, and the third act is when if you're lucky someone will tell you that therapy is available and you have the option of at least treating your Torgo-induced trauma.

Believe it or not, many people who've seen Manos have gone on to live happy, productive lives. Only occasionally has the memory of the horror they witnessed lingered on and flashed before them. Inevitably, they burst into tears and curl up into the fetal position, but the pain soon passes and they go on with their lives. Being forgetful about Manos is the only good kind of Dementia.

Personally, I saw Manos eight or nine times, and in the thirty or so years since, I have experienced great moments of peace and contentment that one time.

I must take a moment to note that I am being a bit insulting to the friends, family and fans who have made me happy on numerous occasions during what is turning out to be a surprisingly long lifetime. And after all these years, I have discovered that friends and family are the only true source of happiness there is, yet happiness has an aloof, elusive quality. When it's not around, which is often, it has a huge power that makes you impatiently anticipate it. It's like a trailer that plays over and over inside your head for a film that you are not convinced is ever going to open. And unfortunately it isn't approved for all audiences.

CHAPTER TWENTY-SEVEN

It is common for a screenplay's first act to end around page 25. So whatever happens to be happening on page 25, that's the end of act one. Yes, I am saying that regardless of what is going on in your story, when you get to page 25, your first act is over, done with, kaput. I know this sounds like I don't know the hell I'm talking about, but you may have already noticed that I'm not very good at this whole screenwriting instruction thing. But this is the inspirational lesson I am trying to leave you with: I didn't let my incompetence stop me from teaching screenplays, so you shouldn't let your incompetence stop you from writing them.

And for God's sake, stick with it, because maybe you're a great talent and the film that is made from your screenplay will alter the consciousness of the world. And if, on the other hand, you do indeed have no talent in the first place, writing something truly shitty will be your ultimate moment of self-actualization.

Either way: do it!

If you're writing the kind of film that might be riffed on *Mystery Science Theater 3000,* the chances are good that there is not a damn thing happening in your screenplay. But writing a script where nothing happens is not without its challenges. To set up a premise where there's no action is one thing, but then sustaining that complete nothingness over the course of an entire "story" is actually quite difficult. The art of cinematic storytelling is rooted in narrative, and nothing is more difficult to pull off than a narrative film where not a damn thing is going on for an hour and a half. But do not worry. It is difficult, but not impossible. Many of the movies that were riffed on *Mystery Science Theater 3000* are completely devoid of action, plot, story and characterization. Yet these films were produced and the writers of these films achieved lasting recognition as people nobody has ever heard of. And all of these screenwriters have IMDB pages, which for all his greatness, never happened to Preston Sturges even once during his lifetime.

But remember, what doesn't happen at the end of your first act is going to drive all of the action that doesn't happen for the rest of the film. You might even have a character say something along the lines of "*Wow! What's happening now is a big deal! This is going to effect the course of our lives for approximately the next hour or so.*" Admittedly, this is a totally hackneyed and obvious way to go, so of course I encourage you to run with it.

But once you've reached act two in your screenplay, you've arrived at the most difficult part of the script to write, so strap yourself in. And I don't mean strap yourself in as a reference to autoeroticism, although choking yourself to enhance your orgasm might be the perfect metaphor for screenwriting, if I were capable of perfect metaphors. And I don't mean strapping something around your arm to shoot-up heroin. Remember, you're a writer, not a musician; a drug habit is not going to make you cool so there's no real value to it.

The second act is the part of your screenplay that will require the most effort, so in many ways it's the opposite of jerking off and shooting up, although the end result will be audience members feeling shame and nodding out, so in that sense the comparison is apt.

F. Scott Fitzgerald, a screenwriter who was also known to dabble in novels and short stories, once said that there are no second acts in American life. What Fitzgerald meant was that America celebrates initial youthful success but is not as excited about older artists following up their earlier efforts with more mature work. I could refute this and list the many writers, musicians and artists who have not allowed their advancing years to prevent them from releasing some of their best output later in their careers, but to be honest I'm pretty tired and my arthritis is acting up, so I'm not feeling up to it right now.

CHAPTER TWENTY-EIGHT

It would be much easier for screenwriters if audiences just watched the first twenty minutes of a film, then went out to get dinner, and then came back for the last ten minutes. This way the middle part of the movie could just be actors sitting around and reading magazines, checking their email and playing cards until the audience returns for the finale and only then would they resume the story.

But alas, this never became the norm. Why? Because audiences hate screenwriters almost as much as producers and movie executives do. Everybody has it in for screenwriters. Everybody.

This might sound harsh, especially because it's not particularly accurate, but if you write scripts and you don't maintain a persecution complex, not to mention a constant boil of simmering recrimination, you risk losing the very essence of what it means to be a screenwriter.

The second act requires the most concentration of any part of your script. That is why you should write it in public venues — a coffee shop, a subway, a strip club, a whore house — any place that provides plenty of distractions. Since the second act is the section of the script that demands the most hours and is the most labor-intensive section of your screenplay, you will need to put more effort into procrastinating.

But once you sit down to do it, writing lots of tedious scenes involving walking, driving and rock climbing is only half the battle. You also have to feel the tedium as you are writing it. Anyone can write a thirty minute scene of an uninteresting character walking through a remote forest, but if you can smell the foot odor waft up from the soles of your shoes as you're writing, it means you're really on to something. It also means that you have serious personal hygiene issues, but either way, you are on the stinky road to being a writer of cheesy movies.

Having no talent is a common trait among a large part of the general population, but harnessing that lack of talent is what separates the amateurs from the amateurish professionals.

A lot of folks go through life blissfully aware that they have no talent. When they watch a great singer, they'll say, "Oh, I could never do that." When they perform karaoke, they gleefully display their lack of talent in public and laugh along with everyone else about how hilarious it is that they suck so much at singing. Most people watch professional athletes knowing that they don't have the talent or skills an ordinary person would need to have access to steroids. They play touch football in the park with full knowledge that they are only doing this as a pretext to get shit-faced drunk at a sports bar afterwards.

But you don't see people engaging in amateur screenwriting on the weekends for fun. No, the place where you see amateur screenwriting on the weekends is your local movie cineplex. Or it might just seem like amateur screenwriting because the writers of these would-be blockbusters had their fine work tossed into a blender by development executives, turning a delightful concoction into a shit smoothy. But regardless of what critics and posters on the Rotten Tomatoes site say about the lack of quality in these films, the screenwriters refuse to see themselves as untalented, and a great many of of them are in fact quite good at their craft. But whether it was marching orders from their employers, or just a natural tendency to conjure cliches and derivative unoriginal stock characters just because it is allowed, they kept writing and never gave up their dreams. And as cheesy as their output is for the rest of us, for them it's meant money, success, and the opportunity to write more cheesy movies for even more money. For many of these writers, the result is a shallow descent into a superficial world of empty sex and decadent materialism, but that doesn't mean there aren't also negative aspects to this situation.

Bit if you really aspire to the life I just described, what I am about to tell

89

you is so important, it can't wait one minute longer.

But I'll get to that later.

CHAPTER TWENTY-NINE

Okay, you put so much of yourself into your second act that it is now finally what you always hoped it would be: a repressed memory that you will never think about again. This means you are ready for the third act, where all the characters that weren't developed can resolve all the conflicts that weren't dramatized.

You are not far from that wonderful day when you can type the words "The End" into your script. Sure, you could have written those words anywhere in the course of your screenplay, but in general, waiting until the last page to write "The End" is how professionals do it. But for a cheesy screenwriter, it's not enough for your movie to end. It has to end inconclusively. Ideally, your movie will be so cheesy, the average viewer will think, "what a waste of money!" even if they watched it as a free download.

But wanting your screenplay to end is only the beginning. As you were writing your script, you were really looking forward to the ending, but all of your cheesy screenwriting will have been in vain if you don't also make the audience look forward to the ending.

Just think of every cheesy movie you've ever seen. Wasn't it a relief when the end finally came? Didn't it seem like a heavy burden had been lifted from you? Like you were now able to put an awful, traumatic experience behind you and move on with your life? Well, it is your job as a writer of cheesy movies to give audience members a traumatic experience that they can eventually feel good about recovering from.

But you have to know when to end a film, and unfortunately, you can't just arbitrarily end a film during whatever happens to be going on when you get to page 90. You can't have a character saying "Well, my point is..." and then put in a freeze frame and roll the credits. That's the kind of shit that happens in a film that's arty, and a cheesy movie is not supposed to be an arty movie. They are both two completely different genres of boring filmmaking.

But give yourself some credit: you somehow managed to figure out a beginning for a story that never got started, and a middle for a plot that never got moving, so maybe now you're ready to write an ending that can't come too soon.

If you are working on an apocalyptic thriller and you can't think of an ending, it's not the end of the world. I bring this up to point out that there are advantages to not having an ending. For one thing, if there's no ending, no one on Twitter can spoil it, although for the kinds of movies I'm talking about, the best way to spoil them is to actually see them.

In recent years, spoilers have become an important part of movie studio marketing campaigns. Generating excitement about a film is the old fashioned form of hype. Ruining the film for everyone before they see it is the modern method of creating buzz.

But your ending can't be spoiled unless you write it first, and now that you've arrived at the third act, the end of your cheesy story might finally be in sight. You've done the hard work of making your script cliched, derivative and one dimensional, and you've awkwardly introduced characters that are so cardboard they've been given UPS tracking numbers. And that's appropriate because you've sent those characters on a journey. You've written long scenes of them driving in cars or walking endlessly through forests. You've sent them towards a destination that would be anticlimactic except that there hasn't been anything in your film that indicated to anyone that anybody was going to reach a climax of any kind.

Occasionally, you may have managed to insert something resembling a storyline or a plot into the proceedings. This is a rookie mistake that many first time cheesy screenwriters make, but don't worry, as your cheesiness grows, things like coherence and clarity will organically fall by the wayside.

Many inexperienced cheesy screenwriters worry about falling into the trap of accidentally entertaining an audience. But that's the beauty of writing on this level. When the bar is set so low that it's fracking at the core of the earth and Mark Ruffalo has organized a protest against it, an uplifting experience is the last thing anyone will expect. You can't ruin an audience's fun when they're not having any in the first place.

If you follow the instructions of this book, there will be no spoilers because something that's already been curdled and covered with mold cannot by it's very nature be spoiled. Crap is mistake-proof in a way that quality never is.

But enjoyment-free cinema is not just confined to low-rent B-movies. There are many expensive, well-made prestige films that are completely lacking in fun, but I've already said enough about the DC Universe. These movies should be an inspiration to all of you who dream of one day seeing your equivalent of "My mother's name is Martha, your mother's name is Martha, let's fight crime together because both our mothers are named Martha" on the big screen. As huge as your cheesy ideas might seem to you now, think of how big and cheesy they'll be when they're on the big IMAX screen. Think of the sense of satisfaction you'll feel watching large groups of irritated movie-goers scratching their heads and muttering "is there a law prohibiting good Fantastic Four movies?" as they leave the theater and angrily throw their 3-D glasses into the recycling bin.

The modern movie business is a whole different ball of cheese than it was back in the era when most of the MST3K-riffed films were made. Most of those movies were originally shown in drive-in theaters or grind houses or not anywhere at all. One of the films we riffed - *The Dead Talk Back* - had its world premiere on *Mystery Science Theater 3000*. There was no red carpet, no spotlights beaming into the sky, no press junket, just a bunch of writers in an industrial park in Eden Prairie, Minnesota laughing to blot out the pain. It was an inauspicious debut — in other words, more than the filmmakers could have dared hope for.

But the 21st century writer of cheesy movies has cause to dream that his or her film might be one of the tentpole blockbuster major studio releases of the summer. Cheesy movies are still B-movies except now they cost hundreds of millions of dollars to make and market, and the fates and careers of thousands of people rests on their success or failure. Think of it: if the cheesy screenplay you write becomes a cheesy movie, the economic security of entire communities will rest on what you wrote. This is the kind of significance a writer of cheesy movies has in the modern era. Face it: you are all-powerful. You are a force to be reckoned with. You are a God. There is nothing wrong with feeling this way about yourself as long as you don't have any delusions of grandeur.

In this day and age, if you are going to suck, suck big. Don't be afraid to fall flat on your face. Your rivals will cheer, but if you get up off the floor and persevere, your success will eventually provide you with enough money for reconstructive facial surgery.

You may worry about how people will feel when they see your film and the words "The End" appear up on the screen. Well, that shouldn't be a concern of yours, because if you do your job as a cheesy screenwriter, most of the audience will have left the theater before the words "The End" appear.

But that's the conundrum of the humdrum: no matter how many hours of meticulous planning go into your cheesy screenplay, you can never determine the exact second when audiences will walk out once it's in a theater. The moment that made you faint from banality while you were writing it could very well end up being the moment that slaps an audience awake and motivates them to stand up and demand a refund.

The nature of art is that it defies expectations and inspires people to do things they weren't expecting to do. This applies to crap as well. Most people thought they would never be in a frame of mind where they would be turned off by the idea of having sex. But then they saw Tommy Wiseau's The Room and suddenly celibacy seemed like a viable option.

Surprisingly, only people who write non-cheesy films can predict when audience members will walk out. You all know who Quentin Tarantino is, right? Of course you do, but he's more than just the star of *Destiny Turns On The Radio*, he also wrote several acclaimed screenplays, including two Academy Award winners, *Pulp Fiction* and *Django Unchained*. And he also wrote *Reservoir Dogs*, knowing darn well that the scene where the kidnapped cop gets his ear cut off would result in at least some walk-outs, and not just from the patrons who were upset that there was no reservoir and not even one dog in the whole damn film. At the time, this was a shocking scene; movie-goers were not as desensitized to violence as they are today, mainly because, unlike current viewers, they hadn't lived through twenty-five years of Quentin Tarantino films. But the point is, when you're watching a cheesy movie, you might not even have the chance to see a guy get his ear cut off because there's a good chance you've already gauged your own eyes out by the time that scene happens.

CHAPTER THIRTY

So let's say you've finally gotten to the end of your script. What now?

Well, I hate to tell you this, but you are not done yet. You have to go back to the beginning and do what is known as a page one rewrite.

But once you've rewritten page one, everything is cool and you can get on with your life.

Oh, wait a minute. That's wrong. Just wishful thinking on my part and I impulsively wrote it down. A page one rewrite means rewriting the entire script from page one until the very end. You may just need to make some cosmetic changes — add a cliche here, remove a stolen idea with a better stolen idea there, or you might need to go over your entire screenplay with a fine tooth toilet scrubber and expand all your endless walking scenes and add dialogue to your many static talky scenes. There could be a moment in the script where you slowed the story down but now upon further reflection you realize that you missed an opportunity to stop the plot altogether. There is no telling how much or how little rewriting your script needs, it mostly depends on your access to opioids.

A rewrite can add depth and nuance to your script, but you should probably do one anyway. However, it's a tricky process. Many amateur screenwriters make the mistake of inserting pointless changes into their scripts way too early; pointless script revisions are central to the Hollywood development process, so that's the type of thing you should leave to professional studio executives who have years of experience ruining scripts.

But you must be analytical about your work. Ask yourself: is that 20 minute sequence where the main character goes to buy beef jerky tedious enough? Should he maybe spend another five minutes deciding which beverage to purchase? Or maybe he could buy a five hour energy drink and you could write a five hour six hundred page scene of him drinking it. Of course, this type of ambitious sequence would be much better suited for a boring mini-series, but you get the idea — these are the types of needed revisions you can spot only in a second draft.

Binge-watching is a popular practice among the general public, so as a writer of cheesy movies you should strive to make your 90 minute film seem like binge-watching. No matter how long or short your film is, a viewer should always feel as if he or she is wasting their time and perhaps even throwing their lives away.

There is an expression in screenwriting circles called "polishing a turd." It means you're refining and changing something that is already a piece of shit. Now, if you were polishing an actual turd, you would get shit all over your hands, but polishing a cinematic turd is a way to get shit up on the movie screen. And if you've ever seen a Transformers movie, you know that sometimes number 2 can be number 1 at the box office.

Ultimately, you might not have what it takes to do a rewrite of your script. You may have already taxed your imagination to the point where you have nothing left to give, and what you've already given may not have been that much in the first place.

So just print out your script and call it a day. Sit back and relax. You deserve to reap the rewards of the half-assed job you've done. The cellular bill for the job you've phoned in has been paid in full. Your work space need not be tidied up because there's no elbow grease to clean. Go ahead and congratulate yourself. Nobody else will.

CHAPTER THIRTY-ONE

Okay, the writing of your cheesy screenplay is done, and after a celebratory visit to your friendly neighborhood crack whore, you are now ready to realize that the hard part of screenwriting is just beginning. I'm talking about the selling of the script. The time has come to cash in on all the hard work you didn't do.

But to sell your script, you are going to have to sell yourself, and you must do it in a creative and inventive way, and that will be quite a task, considering that invention and creativity were never factors during the actual writing of your script. Some writers — the talented ones — express all their creativity on the page, then have none left over when it comes to selling it. But in many cases, writers with no talent for writing are the ones with a real talent for shameless self-promotion. Often people with nothing to sell are really good at selling it, and hopefully you are a regular Willy Loman when it comes to hawking the sample case of nothingness that lies within.

There are many options for selling a screenplay, you just need to figure out which works best for you. Randomly walking up to people on the street and asking them if they'll read your script is not considered professional, and you're also getting ahead of yourself. You don't want to be considered a public nuisance until your movie is released.

Screenplay competitions are one way to go. Unfortunately, the winners of these contests are often picked based on merit, so you can probably cross that option out.

There is an exclusive hierarchy of un-produced screenplays in Hollywood called "The Black List." It is a compilation of un-produced scripts that have impressed the studio executives who've read them. The challenge for the writer of cheesy movies is to somehow get a script noticed that doesn't impress anyone.

The reason screenplays make the Black List is because they have excellent plotting, solid storytelling, deft characterizations and an overall tendency to not suck, so the readers who decide on these things trend to be dickish about screenplays that do suck.

So since there is no possibility that a writer of cheesy movies is ever going to be included on the Black List, you should spend your time focusing on more productive endeavors, like being virulently jealous and resentful towards everyone that is included on the Black List.

They are the cool kids. You are never going to be a cool kid, but that's not necessarily a bad thing. It can be an asset. Not being cool is the fuel that has propelled many careers. It's called Show Business because one of the main motivating thoughts of people who get into it is, "I'll show them!"

But it's hard to show them if they won't read your script in the first place. Many agents won't read a screenplay written by a novice. If you don't already have an established reputation, an agent will have no way of knowing whether he should pretend to be impressed with you or not. Insincerity can be quite exhausting, so agents are choosy when it comes to deciding exactly whom they should smother with fake flattery.

But life is unfair and there's nothing you can do about it, so what's the point of complaining? I long ago accepted this basic fact of life, but do I ever get credit for never complaining about the basic unfairness of life? No! Not ever! I put all this effort into having a healthy, fatalistic attitude about life and what do I get back in return? Nothing! It's such a fucking injustice!

But putting aside the cruelty of a harsh and unforgiving universe for one moment, you have to be proactive and take action that will help you sell your script. Writing a good one was an option but you didn't go that route. So something else has to be figured out.

Are you related to anyone in the movie business? Believe me, if I could teach nepotism, I would have written that book already, but the important thing to remember about nepotism is that it really helps if you're born with it.

I recently found out that one of the cheesiest screenwriters of all time was a product of nepotism. George Worthing Yates, who wrote more movies that were riffed on *Mystery Science Theater 3000* than just about anyone, was the nephew of Herbert Yates, the head of Republic Pictures, a leading maker of cheesy B-movies in the 1930s, 1940s and 1950s. George Worthing Yates' name is on so many MST3K-riffed films that the dripping-with-sarcasm riff, "Oh, is the great George Worthing Yates working on this film" became not just a catchphrase, but more importantly, a catchphrase that never caught on.

Yates worked on serials like *The Phantom Creeps* and then graduated to cheesy classics such as *The Amazing Colossal Man, War of the Colossal Beast, Tormented*, and *Earth Vs. The Spider* (still better than Batman v. Superman).

But dig this, he also worked on *Them!*, a film not riffed on MST3K because we were never offered it, and anyway it was too good for the show, one of the best humongous monster movies of the 1950s.

And the great George Worthing Yates also contributed to the screenplay of a film you may not be familiar with - *The Tall Target*. It's about an assassination attempt on the life of Abraham Lincoln. No, not the assassination that you've all heard off, the commercial, mainstream, inside-the-beltway assassination that happened at the Ford Theater. That one is well known because John Wilkes Booth was an actor who understood the importance of milking publicity. No, The Tall Target was a true story about another, earlier plot to kill Lincoln. (Don't quite know why I had to point out it was an "earlier" assassination plot. An attempt to kill Lincoln after he was already assassinated by Booth would have been kind of besides the point.)

The Tall Target starred Dick Powell as real life Pinkerton detective John Kennedy. (Yes, his actual name! I'll never forget where I was when I heard that John Kennedy was his real name.)

It was directed by Anthony Mann, who made all those great 1950s Westerns with Jimmy Stewart, and it's an excellent thriller. It is genuinely suspenseful even though we know that the plot to kill Lincoln won't succeed, this time at least. Sometimes History needs to come with a spoiler warning

Try and catch it next time it's on Turner Classic Movies and give a tip of the stovepipe hat to George Worthing Yates. He's a member of the cheesy screenwriting hall of fame, but sometimes when it comes to a person's talent, there's more than meets the cheese.

But right now some of you may have turned on your sarcasm sequencer and are saying, "Oh, is the great George Worthing Yates going to take up this entire chapter..."

(Pause... pause... pause... Sorry, I was waiting for that catchphrase to catch on. It didn't happen this time either.)

Continuing your thought: "...Screw the great George Worthing Yates! What about me and my career? How do I sell my cheesy screenplay?"

Well, I've got some good news. There are practical options.

For instance, why not pick the agent you feel is best suited for you and then kidnap one of his or her relatives?

Admittedly, extorting a human life for agency representation has its impractical side. For one thing, if you send the agent a package with your victim's severed limb, you might get back a note saying, "sorry, we don't accept unsolicited material." And if you call the agent's office with your ransom demand, good luck getting your call returned.

At most, maybe the agent's assistant will read your ransom note and then the agent will read the assistant's coverage of your demands, and the assistant's coverage will probably say something along the lines of, "this ransom demand is contrived and derivative. Although your kid brother is in imminent danger of a gruesome death, the kidnapper really needs to raise the stakes. I recommend we pass."

This is a harsh truth, but it's just the reality of the situation: getting an agent is hard, even if you terrorize and harm his loved ones. As has been noted before, life is unfair.

Before you send your script to an agent, you might consider showing it to friends and colleagues. It is important for a writer to surround him or herself with a community of writers. There's a wonderful back-and-forth that occurs among the fellowship of scribes — any success that you have is a failure for them and any success that they have confirms your worst fears about yourself. And don't forget, every honor that someone else receives is a declaration that you never should have been allowed to have dreams in the first place. But that isn't to say you don't have purpose, because you can always take comfort knowing that your failures are giving hope and inspiration to others.

These are the kinds of thoughts that can contaminate a writer's mind and prevent him or her from doing the work that needs to get done. I've been infected with notions such as these for my entire life but I wanted to share them with you as a way of giving back.

A writer needs to keep his feet firmly planted on the ground, but if you allow your mind to be weighted down by petty bullshit, your feet will end up being firmly planted in quick sand. If you stay focused on your work and don't worry about the fortunes or failures of others, you are more likely to succeed and have the rich, satisfying life you've always wanted.

But where's the fun in that?

CHAPTER THIRTY-TWO

Just as a disease needs to escape its host to spread its contagious virus throughout the world, you have send your cheesy script out and away from your computer so that the movie-going public can one day come down with a severe case of your work.

Over a period of several months, you gave a whole week of your life to writing your screenplay. You can't let all that effort go to waste. If you die without a script being produced, your name will be forgotten by history, almost as forgotten as the names of those who have had their scripts produced.

That's why I've been emphasizing the importance of aggressive self-promotion. You know those people who sell jewelry on the Home Shopping Network? That jewelry is every bit as cheesy as your screenplay, and yet there they are, selling their wares as if cubic zirconia was a real life blood diamond elegant enough to cause actual misery in the world. That's the kind of positive attitude you need to have. Tackiness and salesmanship are a potent combination. If you believe you are vulgar, you will be vulgar. Release the pink plastic flamingo within and let it soar!

And don't forget, successful mediocrities with no talent all have one thing in common — they believe in themselves.

There are lots of examples I could give you of real geniuses - Van Gogh, Kafka, Kurt Cobain - who had no faith in their own abilities and even less self-esteem. These traits are common among truly great artists, so if you are shallow and one-dimensional with a bubblegum brain, count yourself lucky that you don't suffer the torture of being great.

Writing is at its heart a spiritual practice. After all, where does inspiration come from? If you're a writer of cheesy movies, it frequently comes from other writers, but where do they get their ideas?

God?

Perhaps. Many believers say that God is Good. It is a catchphrase among religious people, and unlike "Oh, is the great George Worthing Yates going to deliver us from evil," "God is Good" is a catchphrase that has actually caught on.

Well, if the highest praise the supreme deity of the entire universe can inspire from his fans is "good," it means that even the creator of all mankind can't inspire superlatives, so don't expect much critical praise for the shit you're doing.

But there are many ways for a writer to get attention. You can stand at a movie studio gate and light yourself on fire, but this is impractical because however much of an impact your self-immolation may have, you'll never get a follow up meeting.

How about paying someone off? Giving a reader or a studio development executive money to read your script and give good coverage of it? I'm afraid this is untenable because most writers trying to break in are too broke for bribery, and unfortunately I can tell you from personal experience that Arby's coupons are not an effective form of coercion.

It is frustrating to write a script that meets all the requirements of cheesy cinema yet is not playing on the big screen. A world that has room for a Baywatch movie ought to have room for your cheesy movie. Hard as it is to believe, there are incidents in recorded human history when actual human beings approached box office windows said, "Yes, I'll have two tickets for *Battlefield Earth*, please." And yet your cheesy screenplay was rejected not just by Hollywood, but by your cat, who wouldn't even use your hard copy as a scratching post. Everyone's a critic.

Artists suffer for their art. What you suffer for is anybody's guess, but suffering is suffering no matter how talented or untalented you are. As Patrick Swayze said in *Roadhouse*, "Pain don't hurt." And that is as pointless a thing to say now as it was then.

But you'd better brace yourself, because I'm about to give you some harsh truths about the entertainment industry that you might not want to hear, but better that you hear it from me than from someone who knows what they're talking about.

I hate to tell you this, but Hollywood is filled with prejudice and discrimination. Many women are not hired because of their gender, and people of color are not employed at nearly the level they should be. White men are hired at a much higher rate, but that is because white men are better at cashing in on their mediocrity than other races. Many woman, however talented, didn't have the savvy to be be born with a penis Of course these days it's possible for anyone to have a male organ, but even a woman with a newly acquired dick is still at a disadvantage when it comes to winning pissing contests.

So now you might be wondering, what's the problem with the author of this book? I'm a white male. I have a penis, and I've even used it once or twice. So how come I'm not writing blockbuster movies?

Well, it's partly because I'm 61 and that's considered old by Hollywood standards. But my age has had no effect on my writing whatsoever.

So how come I'm not writing blockbuster movies?

Well, it's partly because I'm 61 and that's considered old by Hollywood standards. But my age has had no effect on my writing whatsoever.

So how come I'm not writing blockbuster movies?

Well, it's partly because I'm 61 and that's considered old by Hollywood standards. But my age has had no effect on my writing whatsoever.

Also, it's partly because I'm 61 and that's considered old by Hollywood standards. But my age has had no effect on my writing whatsoever.

Another reason might be because I'm 61 and that's considered old by Hollywood standards. But my age has had no effect on my writing whatsoever.

I also think it partly has to do with the fact that I'm 61 and that's considered old by Hollywood standards. But my age has had no effect on my writing whatsoever.

Okay, I have to go have a difficult bowel movement now, but before I do, let me lay another harsh reality on you. While Hollywood makes many movies that are indeed quite bad, they still somehow have the notion that they should hire good writers who are actually talented and excel at what they do. Like just about everything in the movie business, this makes absolutely no sense. If they're going to make a cheesy movie, why not just hire a cheesy writer? But the assholes who run film studios do everything ass-backwards. Rather than hire a cheesy writer who feels totally comfortable writing a cheesy movie, they instead hire a good writer who feels his soul slipping away as a million studio notes from a dozen development executives turn something that might have been okay into something not very good. For film studios, it's much more satisfying to crush the dreams of an artist than to realize the dreams of a hack. Hiring a cheesy writer in the first place would eliminate the middle man, but Hollywood never does things efficiently.

That's the problem with the entertainment industry. There are all kinds of executives who stand between writers and their films. True, there are always several instances every year where the result of this process is an entertaining movie, sometimes even a film of great artistic merit. But what the hell does that have to do with what we're talking about in this book?

In a fair and just world, bad movies would only enrich bad writers, instead of enriching good writers who feel bad about the under-par work they become associated with. It would also help if talented writers displayed integrity and refused to work on artistically compromised projects; this would make it much easier for those who are downright eager to whore themselves.

The truth is, cheesy writers can be just as passionate about their work as non-cheesy writers If any kind of writer puts his or her heart and soul into their screenplay, the writing itself will nourish the heart and soul of the person doing the writing. The sense of accomplishment from having done it in the first place will fill them with pride.

Which will only make it that much more painful when Hollywood takes all that passion and grinds it through the de-passion-izer. Writers of every stripe, on every level, will often see their writing get diluted by the studio system, and even if the movie gets made, it usually ends up being something someone casually watches, only to shrug and say, "yeah, that was okay, I guess," and some writers give their all to write the best screenplay they can, and then the most common reason anyone watches their film is because "there was nothing else on." Other writers, the less ambitious kind, write the films that are the "nothing" in "nothing else on."

Writers, filmmakers, actors, cinematographers, editors and all sorts of artisans and technicians put a tremendous amount of effort into the making of a movie. Sometimes it turns out great, other times not so much. But regardless of the outcome, there is always a great deal of passion involved, and in honor of that passion, I will make a real point of watching those films if I happen to be around when they come on basic cable at 3 in the morning.

Storytelling is an ancient art, it goes all the way back to cavemen sitting around campfires and telling tales to the women they forcibly dragged into their caves. These days, no one can be forced into a movie theater, which is why the Tom Cruise Mummy movie didn't do as well as many had hoped.

My point is that every year Hollywood makes movies that are instantly forgotten the moment people are through watching them. Someone has to write those films, so why shouldn't it be you? There is nothing better than touching another human being with your art. But in lieu of that, why not become a writer of cheesy movies?

Is a career in cheesy screenwriting just a dream? It's been said that a dream is a wish your heart makes; in your case, that dream might be a wish your taint makes, but who cares? A dream is a dream is a dream. Your ship may be coming in any day now. In all likelihood that ship will be a *Carnival of Souls* Cruise Line overflowing with food poisoning and legionaries disease, but your cheesy movie will be the playing in that ship's multiplex, and as you watch the viewers of your film doubled over, grabbing their stomachs, vomiting and shitting their pants, you will know that you have shared your gift with the world.

Remember, the cream always rises to the top, something that will become clear to you as you serve coffee at Starbucks for the rest of your life.

But never let anyone crush your dream. A great screenplay will break through the muck and stand out from the pack. There will always be a place for genius in this world, but never let that discourage you.

Made in the USA
San Bernardino, CA
12 December 2017